W9-BTQ-577

IT WAS ME
ALL ALONG

IT WAS ME ALL ALONG

a memoir

ANDIE MITCHELL

clarkson potter/publishers
new york

Published in the United States by Clarkson Potter/Publishers,
an imprint of the Crown Publishing Group,
a division of Random House LLC,
a Penguin Random House Company, New York.
www.crownpublishing.com
www.clarksonpotter.com

CLARKSON POTTER is a trademark
and POTTER with colophon is a registered trademark
of Random House LLC.

Grateful acknowledgment is made to Kenneth Carroll for permission to reprint
"Elaborate Signings" from *So What: For the White Dude Who Said This Ain't Poetry*
(The Bunny & Crocodile Press, 1997). Reprinted by permission of the author.

Library of Congress Cataloging-in-Publication Data
Mitchell, Andie.
It was me all along / Andie Mitchell.
pages cm
1. Mitchell, Andie. 2. Overweight women—Anecdotes. 3. Obesity in women—
Psychological aspects. 4. Lifestyles—Health aspects. I. Title.
RC552.O25.M58 2015
616.3'98—dc23
2013036057

ISBN 978-0-7704-3324-6
eBook ISBN 978-0-7704-3326-0

Printed in the United States of America

Book design by Ashley Tucker
Jacket design by Stephanie Huntwork
Jacket photography courtesy of the author

2 4 6 8 10 7 5 3 1

First Edition

For my mother. Everything I am is because of you.

IT WAS ME
ALL ALONG

introduction

IF YOU WERE NOT ABLE TO ATTEND my twentieth birthday party, you missed a fabulous cake.

And if, by chance, you were able to attend my twentieth birthday party, you, too, missed a fabulous cake.

In fact, everyone did, save for me.

I can remember carving the first slice, taking the first forkful. The rush of whipped sugar speeding through my bloodstream. It felt like teetering on the ledge on the roof of a skyscraper, exhilarating and terrifying. The split-second decision between balance and oblivion.

What I cannot remember, however, is the exact moment I made the decision to eat the whole thing.

Scraping the sides of the mixing bowl, I began to notice just how satiny the fudge batter was. I made swirls and figure eights with my spatula. In transferring heaping spoonfuls of espresso-hued chocolate cream to the cake tins, I reveled in the lightness of texture, the airiness of what I was working with. A scoop in the pan, a scoop in the mouth. I then watched through the oven door as the cakes materialized, rising to fill their nine-inch pans.

Ten minutes into the baking, the air in my apartment was so saturated with the aroma of chocolate that I lost the ability to focus on anything but that cake. Though I had already eaten lunch and cake batter, a new hunger appeared, unexpected and urgent, the kind that forced me to stop whatever I was doing and tend to it. It was the kind I couldn't ignore, the one that wrestled away my power, every hidden weapon of will, and thrust me into the kitchen, where it always seemed I'd run out of milk and self-control.

While the cake cooled, I bided time by making the frosting, following the same rigorous taste-testing protocol as I had with the cake. Once my mixing bowl was full of glossy stiff peaks, I iced both layers. I carved one perfect slice, dragging my index finger along the flat side of the knife to collect any wayward fudgy crumbs, and brought it to my mouth for a thorough licking. I ate the slice of cake with fervor, as if intently pursuing something. I devoured a second slice, and then a third, trailed hastily by another three. I carved one more, reasoning that would just about do it, but, oh—look at the crooked edge I'd produced with my shoddy knife skills. A sliver more would straighten it. I whittled away at the frosting, and, finally sure that enough was enough, I walked away from the cake and laid my fork and knife in the sink. I turned back to the cake stand and, in one painful glance, saw all that remained. A single slice.

Guilt has a way of resisting digestion. There's nothing natural about its aggressive spread. It stretches out inside me, doubles its size by uncurling its chubby arms and legs. It kicks and groans every slip of the way down. It reminds me, shames me, at every twist, every turn. And when it plops down at last upon the base of my stomach, it stays for days, unwelcome.

When it finally begins to dissolve in a halfhearted effort to leave me, particles of self-hatred remain. And hatred, like acid, erodes the whole of its environment.

What begins as hating the cake for all its multiple layers of luscious temptation spirals quickly into hating myself and all my fat cells. I let myself down. I lament not having more control. I crave comfort and reassurance, but the shame pushes me to choose punishment instead; it's all I deserve. And though crying seems a valid option, tears elude me. Instead, I stay stuck internally, bottled and sealed inside my own skin with the acidity of hatred and guilt and shame.

Today, eight years later, I'm standing again at my kitchen counter, tending to the same fudge cake. I'm gently lowering the top layer onto its frosting pillow. I've baked this cake enough times that I don't even have to take a bite to know the rich velvet of its texture. It has always been decadent, always as intense as a square of high-quality dark chocolate. A forkful makes me know that, were I able to suspend hot fudge in air just long enough to hold it and bite into it, just to taste it during the moments before it oozed, thick on my tongue, it'd be the same as this cake.

And then there's the frosting: a whipped confection with a texture that lies somewhere between the airiness in a cloud of cotton candy and the fluffy marshmallow filling in a 3 Musketeers candy bar.

Swiping a finger through that frosting, I stop. I consider how wildly my feelings about eating this one cake have swung in the last seven years. Since that time, I have lost 135 pounds. The weight has left my body and, with it, the guilt, the shame, and the hatred, too. I think briefly of the days when the very sight of a confection induced a seductive fantasy of eating it all in secret. Maybe it's knowing that I could get away with it, the acknowledgment that I could eat it all without anyone ever seeing me do it, that gives me pause today.

I am a lifetime practitioner of secretive eating, after all. As a kid who entered an empty house after school each day, I felt a desperation to eat. I knew no way other than eating to alleviate the loneliness, to fill in the spaces where comfort and security could have been. Food poured over the millions of cracks in the foundation of my family; it seeped into the fissures; it narrowed the chasms. But even then I knew that the amount of food I was consuming was something to be ashamed of. So I learned to hide it well. I stuffed twin packs of Little Debbie Swiss Cake Rolls deep inside my stomach, tightly tucking them away. I plunged their cellophane wrappers even deeper inside the trash can, where they couldn't be seen without digging.

Until the year of my twentieth birthday, I lugged around the heavy shame of my eating. I'd devour a steak-and-cheese sandwich on the way home to eat dinner with my family. I'd find myself two days into a new diet, alone in my car, pulling through the drive-through window of the Burger King two towns over—the one where I was certain no one would recognize me. I'd griddle three stacks of pancakes in the mornings after Mom had left for work, stab my fork into the thick, cakey center of each one, and then slosh the bite through puddles of maple syrup and melted butter.

But today, eating ceaselessly in private doesn't lure me the way it once did. It doesn't seduce me in the same sexy way. In fact, there were years after having lost one-hundred-plus pounds when the sight of this fudge cake didn't conjure up fantasy, but fear—a few birthdays when I spent the hours and days leading up to the cake searching my mind desperately for ways to escape eating it. I thought of excuses. I thought of ways to chew the cake in front of friends and family and spit it out in my napkin in the privacy of the next room. Three birthdays came and went without my so much as licking the frosting that touched my fingers while icing the layers.

The thinness I'd achieved came with its own brand of indignity. It was the fear of gaining back each pound, of proving myself a failure, that plagued me. It was the fatness of my shadow that followed me into the dark alley of an eating disorder. And just as I always had, I stuffed the shame so far down that no one could see it but me. For the first time, I appeared healthy on the outside. I wanted badly to conceal the fact that, despite a radical transformation, I remained as screwed up as I had ever been.

I lied about just having eaten to eschew offers of food at the dinner table with my family. I drove in circles in my neighborhood, unsure of how to fill the hours on an empty stomach. I bought snacks I had no intention of eating when I went to the movie theater with friends. I doggie-bagged the leftovers at restaurants, only to plunge them into the trash can the moment I arrived home. Even after rekindling my passion for baking, I restricted myself to the smallest of portions and gave the rest away.

Making this cake now, a few years later, I see how starkly black and white my beliefs had been. I see the tragedy in living an all-or-nothing existence, in teetering on top of that skyscraper and feeling forced to choose between standing paralyzed in fear or hurling myself over the edge in ecstasy. I recognize the pain of white-knuckling my way through life. I recognize the internal chaos of barreling through life in bouts of mania and depression. The alternative, the middle ground, is balance. It's not wishing to stay or to fall; it's remaining upright, respecting the boundary of the rooftop and admiring the exhilaration, the strength, of standing so high.

By now I've changed dramatically. I can, I want to, I choose to eat a full slice of this cake and love deeply all the many bites I take. I linger on the cocoa flavor, the suede texture, and, when one piece has reached its clean-plate end, I don't look for another to replace it. I share this cake. I eat it out in the open, in a loud and proud manner. I take pride in having baked something so rich, so true and divine. I won't eat until I can no longer feel anything but the stretching of my stomach, the growing of my guilt.

Every year since losing all the weight, I've baked this sour cream fudge cake. And every year, I've felt different about the finished product. How has one innocent cake transformed from abusive lover to healthy companion, while I've continued to bake it just the same?

Has the taste changed, or, perhaps, have I?

1

SHE ALWAYS LET ME LICK THE BEATERS FIRST.

I grasped the spindly handle of the beater, top-heavy with slick sand-colored dough, and brought it to my mouth as I might an ice cream cone. I grinned into each lick, the corners of my mouth widening into a smile and my tongue extending around each curved silver wire. Gritty brown sugar dissolving; the velvetiness of feather-light flour beaten into softened butter. Of all the tastes I've stashed in my memory, that of my mother's chocolate chip cookies may linger longest. Like her, the flavor is assertive and distinct. As definitive as her Boston accent.

I continued licking, noting her signature doubling of chocolate chips. She looked down and ran her fingers—rough as sandpaper from years of cleaning the homes of others—through the chaos of black curls sprouting on my head. And with her touch I was somehow bothered, mostly by the disruption of such happy licking. I returned her gaze, just in case she was considering taking that precious beater from my pudgy right palm, and I saw her own hair, wet and as ebony as mine, sneaking out from under a towel. Moments out of a nearly sterilizing hot shower, she was always trying to get four things done at once.

When my eyes caught hers, she puckered her lips and leaned down to kiss me. She pulled back, lingering a moment to remind me, "Francie, I love you ever ever over, even under dirty filthy water."

I never knew exactly what that phrase meant. Not the name she called me, certainly not the rest. But I understood that this was her way of telling my brother and me we were her lifeblood. It was her unique way of saying "I love you more than anything in this world."

I smiled and returned my focus to that battered beater.

"What else do we need for the party?" she asked earnestly.

She twirled around, assessing the platters, plates, and trays covering every last centimeter of tiled counter space. The table unable to be set with linens or silverware because the food couldn't spare the space. The chairs, each with a sweet on its seat. Stacks of plates, cloth napkins rolled and ringed with gold, coolers of cubed ice studded with cans of soda and beer.

"Just cake!" I said, and squealed with delight.

She always made birthdays a grand affair, with balloons and big, boisterous decorations. Never one without an eighteen-inch triple-layer cake from Daniel's Bakery, our then-favorite cake shop, an hour away. This year's party was no different, Mom reminded me. "Of course we've got cake, baby."

The very thought of more sweets sweetened me. Still working my tongue through sugar-meets-butter pre-cookie, I looked around at the spread she'd prepared with me at her side. Deli platters sat coupled with their fluffy bakery rolls, meatballs stewed in marinara with links of spicy sausage bulging like panty hose around an overflowing thigh, trays of lasagna so piping hot, the cheese blistered and the sauce bubbled beyond each pan's border. Freshly baked bread with seven sticks of butter softening alongside. Bowls heaping with grated Parmesan cheese set beside soupspoons for sprinkling. The hors d'oeuvres—the homemade crackers cut into precise squares, chicken pâté, a dip to plunge every chip in— were kept quarantined in the breezeway. And then, the dessert. No fewer than three fruit pies, each a deep blue, mauve, or red staining her homemade all-butter pastry; two dozen of her thick-like-fudge brownies; custard-filled mini éclairs from the New Paris Bakery in Brookline; those relentlessly chewy chocolate chip cookies; and that special layer cake.

It seemed a reasonable buffet to serve thirty of our family members.

Ever the beloved party-thrower, Mom stayed true to her three trusted modes of catering: massive, more massive, and most massive.

But we're a family of eaters, all of us, and eaters eat well. We like multiple options. We take comfort in knowing we can always cleanse our palates with deep-dish apple pie before moving on to birthday cake. We think about parties first in terms of menu, followed closely by dessert buffets. I trace this obsession with abundance back to Mom's mom—a collector. She held on to used wrapping paper as tightly as she did grudges. She saved food, possessions, and incidentals. Her tendency to keep a well-stocked fridge and freezer packed with wartime-like rations years after all her nine babies had left the nest was likely the result of a gene trickled down from an ever-starving Irish family. And my mother, the second oldest of nine, is forever scared of scarcity. It's knitted into the fiber of her warm woolen soul to gather and provide for anyone who needs providing.

To this day, Mom serves food in the manner she loves: in heaps and sloppy gobs and spilling surplus. She pays no mind to amount or frequency or even what slight portion she may be able to save for herself; she just gives. Unconditional and fierce, she works optimally with excess. She hugs tightly, presses a kiss on your lips like a heavily inked red stamp, buys bulk in bulk, speaks and acts with Broadway-stage gusto, smears butter on her bread generously, and, if you ask her for anything—anything at all—she'll make it so.

My fifth birthday party was a classic example of her aim to please. She'd made every dish that I—a food fanatic at five—knew existed. The scale of platters alone minimized all the buffets we'd ever seen. I truly could not think of an item she hadn't already prepared and plated.

And still, she bit the side of her lip, unsure. "You think this is enough?" Her hands clamped at her waist as she swiveled once more to assess the food.

"Yep," I replied.

"Have a cupcake while you wait."

Without hesitation I marched to the table, three giddy breaths away. Tippy-toeing so that my eyes just surfaced over the table's wooden ledge, I looked lovingly at the plate she had carefully assembled that morning: pale pink parchment cups polka-dotted with lavender, each puffed with dainty coconut cake. I scanned the dozen, determined to find the one with the fullest frosting cloud.

I knew what kind of standards one should uphold with baked goods: frosting on cupcakes should sit no less than two fingerwidths high; cookies should be crackled across their tops to reveal gooey, barely baked centers; the best piece of sheet cake is always the corner and, of course, sporting a frosting rose. I had a discerning sweet tooth—several of them, I imagine.

At this age, I was sweetly appled, cute, and roly-poly, standing three-and-a-half feet tall and weighing sixty pounds. I remember my fondness for that appropriately garnet-hued January birthday dress. The stiff collar of ruffled velvet, the empire waist and poufed hoop skirt. A twirl and a polite curtsy every few minutes emphasized how regal, how happily fancy-schmancy I felt at the time. I pirouetted in front of the hall mirror and saw my brother at my back, heading toward his room.

At eleven years old, Anthony was constantly running around. From sunup to sundown, he was outside, playing sports with his friends, while I was inside, mostly sitting and often alone. People told him he took after Mom's side of the family. "So tall and skinny!" they'd say. And then they'd look at me—big and round—and note my resemblance to Dad.

I picked up my coconut cupcake—the one heaviest in buttercream love—and made my way to the next room. There on our navy floral couch, still pajamaed and groggy, sat Dad. I surveyed him carefully, knowing how sour his moods usually were in the morning and early afternoon.

"Hi, baby." He smiled, motioning for me to sit beside him. I was relieved and surprised that he was so upbeat so early in the day. *He must be making today special because of my party,* I thought as I took a seat.

"Happy birthday." He bent toward me to press a big smooch

on my temple. He squeezed me in his bearish way, and I smiled a closed-mouth smile, leaning into him. I peeled the oily paper lining from my cupcake and set about savoring it.

He had just gotten up, half an hour before the party guests were due to arrive. Twelve thirty in the afternoon wasn't an unusual wake-up time for him. Nights spent drinking beer can after beer can after beer can after beer can, can, can, can, can don't lend well to early rising the following day. I didn't know that all dads weren't consistent in buying two six-packs of those red-and-white cans at the liquor store up the street and coming home to drink and chain-smoke in front of *M*A*S*H* until the sun came up. It was normal for us. Still, I wondered why he was so thirsty all the time. I wondered if it was just so delicious, he didn't want to stop. One time, when he left the room and I saw his beer can open on the counter unattended, I rushed up and took a swig to see if it tasted as good as Nesquik. It didn't.

Weeks before, Mom had told me that Dad had lost his job. Understandably, he was crushed. He moped around the house even worse than he'd done regularly. For years, he'd held a meaningful, well-paying position as a technical illustrator at Wang Laboratories, a computer company close to where we lived in Methuen, Massachusetts. Always an artist, creative and dramatic, he was brilliant. I remember going to work with him on days before school started and sitting at his desk, coloring in the black-and-white illustrations of the many small parts inside a computer. Even as an adult, reading instruction manuals whenever I get a new camera, computer, or phone and seeing those precise pictures of the inner technology and parts, I'm reminded of the contentment I felt in his office with a box of crayons, working away at what you'd think must have been the driest of coloring-book material.

"Almost party time," Dad reminded me.

"Uh-huh," I mumbled through my cupcake, dropping crumbs in my lap.

He ashed his cigarette and turned forward.

As I neared the end of the cupcake, I thought of the big cake in the dining room. I felt relieved that my birthday cake sat still intact and safe. Just six months earlier, Dad had eaten Anthony's the night before the party, drunk and with his bare hands. I thought of how devastated I'd be if that cake were mine.

From the kitchen, Mom hollered, "Rob, you should get dressed, honey. People are going to start showing up any minute."

Dad exhaled a cloud of smoke. He stubbed his cigarette into the translucent green glass bottom of one of the four heavy ashtrays we kept around the house. He rocked back and then forth, rising on the upswing to heave his 350 pounds to standing. The weight proved to be all he gained after losing his job.

"Whooo boy!" he exclaimed emphatically. "Let's get ready, baby." He smiled at me.

I stuffed the last of the cupcake into my mouth before I repaid his exuberance by getting up myself. As I rose, I watched him—a solid five-foot-ten frame stretching outward in an all-encompassing yawn. He had silky jet-black hair, golden skin, and almond eyes that cracked open as he smiled. He barely had a top lip. The pronounced structure of his face—high cheekbones, deep-set eyes— was so handsome, it proved striking, unforgettable.

He bent to kiss my forehead, hard and purposeful, once more. I trailed him as he headed into the kitchen.

Coming up from behind Mom, he wrapped his arms tightly around her waist, pressing his nose to her hair, breathing her in. Her body softened, nuzzling backward into his chest. She craned her neck back, turning so that she could smile looking into his eyes. He glanced down, assessing her lips before planting a kiss squarely upon them.

They loved each other, of that much I was sure. As the story goes, they met in high school, the day he hopped into her car with a big group of friends. She eyed him from the rearview mirror, unsure what to make of him. He was overwhelming, taking up nearly all of the car with his ego. Joke after joke spit from his mouth at the expense of their mutual friends in the backseat. Mom glanced back, unamused. By the end of the drive, she thought he was a jerk, she tells me now, and she'd written him off after that first afternoon.

Weeks later they saw each other at her all-girls-school dance, each with a date. What made it hard to completely dislike him was the fact that she found him gorgeous. Toward the end of the evening, Mom found herself staring toward the left of the dance floor, where a classmate of hers stood all alone. The girl looked uncomfortable, less a wallflower and more a weed in olive-green taffeta. Seeing her there, swaying by herself without even a single suitor all night, with her gaze wandering the room for someone—anyone— Mom's heart felt heavy. She thought to ask the girl to dance herself, and before really mulling it over, Mom picked up the hem of her dress and took a step toward her. Suddenly Dad passed in front of her, headed straight toward the girl. Mom watched as he approached. Something he said into her ear made her laugh, made her nerves gently unravel. A smile spread across Mom's face as she realized he'd asked the girl to dance. And she couldn't peel her eyes away as they swayed there on the dance floor to Marvin Gaye.

"You thought he was cute," I'd assumed when Mom told me the

story of that dance. She paused and thought on it, looking away as if an answer were just over her shoulder.

"No, it wasn't that. I mean—yes, obviously—look at him! But that night, it was just—I hadn't seen the girl smile like that before."

She gave him a chance after that night. And eventually he grew on her. She found his gentle underbelly, and then she felt special, imagining he let only her see the intimate parts of him—the gifted artist, brimming with insight and intuition, with a deep-running sensitivity.

When I'd matured enough to ask Dad about how they met and fell in love, he didn't wait a beat to tell me that from the moment he got into her car, he just knew. He explained to me the meaning of soul mates and then told me that he and Mom were such a pair. Her honesty, her sincerity—they disarmed him. "Just the way she talked to everyone," he began a list that included the way she always offered to be the sober driver; how she'd invite everyone to the drive-in and bring homemade sandwiches, chips, Ring Dings, and Cokes; that she worked two jobs, one at St. Elizabeth's Hospital and one at Friendly's; how she'd slip twenty dollars into her father's pants pocket while he napped on the chair after his fifth night shift in a row; how she'd never gotten drunk after that first time she had gin, when she came home a mess and her father told her he was disappointed; and how Mom would undoubtedly give someone the shirt off her back.

Dad saw these things and loved them. He'd never met anyone like Mom. Five months after they'd begun dating, he tattooed her initials, *MEC*, with a razor blade and ink, on his forearm. He was that sure of her.

And I grew to recognize that spark they shared. It was wild and unruly at times but always unconditional. No one made her laugh in as high a pitch. No one made his eyes soften as they did when he looked at her.

Mom turned back to her preparations, pulling out of their embrace. "OK, but seriously, Rob. Time to get ready."

"I'm gonna wear this," he told her.

She smirked.

"What?" he asked, straight-faced. He backed away from her so she could stare at the full length of him, in his underwear, and turned slowly to show off.

We both laughed.

He slapped her butt, kissed her once more, and left for the bedroom.

I looked at Mom. She was still bouncing in a laugh, shaking her head as she walked into the bathroom. I waited to hear her hair dryer purr. In seconds, she was midway through her familiar whistle, a tune she had shared with her father. The cupcakes caught me again, sitting on their porcelain plate. I smiled, knowing no one was around to stop me from taking another. I inspected each once more, zeroing in on the most generously frosted. My mouth tingled with sweet anticipation as I pulled the winner carefully from its center spot and began peeling back the pleated parchment cup. The first bite gave me a rush. Mom had a way with cake. Each crumb was stitched to the next, a soft and silky webbing between moist bites. I opened my mouth wider to fit more frosting, more cake. It was that familiar combination—the subtly fragrant cake mashing into a smooth paste with ultrasmooth vanilla buttercream—that I loved, that I craved.

I plowed through the rest. My tongue ran a tight circle around my mouth to help dissolve every remainder of richness. Finishing it brought a wave of contentment, a wash of relief. Two cupcakes—gone. Eaten.

But the number of treats I downed meant very little to me. What difference existed between two and one of anything? Calories, moderation, health—they weren't even a consideration of mine. Not then. I didn't pause to consider hunger and fullness; I just ate.

In an ideal world, a child learns eating as an intuitive practice. She seeks out and savors what she wants when she feels hungry. She stops when her stomach sends signals to her brain to say "Hello, hi, I've had enough." Gentle bodily sensations are the sole systems she needs to rely on.

I learned none of that. Food was never simply fuel. It was never just about hunger, and it certainly didn't stop at fullness.

My earliest teacher was Dad, and he ate ceaselessly through the night. In fact, he only ate at night. After drinking. In between slurps of his six-pack while lying in bed in front of Nick at Nite, he'd *mmmm* his way through a large steak-and-cheese sub and a bag of potato chips, our favorite kettle-cooked kind. When he'd finished those, he'd return to the kitchen to pluck his favorite from the freezer: a half gallon of some generic tub of whatever the grocery store called vanilla ice cream with chocolate chips.

He was markedly happier at night. Goofy and unbothered by anything. I learned to count the red-and-white cans that he'd crush between his big hands. I knew that three of them in the trash meant Dad would be fun soon. After four, he'd be hungry. Wanting to be with him while he ate, I'd get hungry, too. Eating was special. I'd lie there and nibble beside him in their king-size bed well past midnight, both enjoying and feeling guilty for all the space on Mom's side—vacant because she was at work. We'd watch our nightly roster of shows: *Andy Griffith, Bewitched, The Dick Van Dyke Show.* By one thirty, he'd have smoked a full pack of Kool 100's beside me before falling into a deep sleep. Just as I drifted, too, I'd wake to see Anthony beside the bed, carefully pulling a lit cigarette from between Dad's fingers and stubbing it in the ashtray. He'd then come around to my side of the bed and kiss my cheek before turning off the TV.

On weekend mornings, I'd wake up early and know Dad was hours from rising. Anthony was off at baseball, as usual. If it wasn't baseball, it was football. And if not football, basketball, or street hockey. Always something, somewhere, until dark. Like Mom, he used an alarm clock and had keys to the front door. I'd walk to the kitchen, independent and capable, and climb onto the counter to get to the cereal cabinet. When I'd chosen from among Lucky Charms, Corn Pops, Cap'n Crunch, and Frosted Flakes, I'd pull the box down and go about fetching a bowl, a soupspoon, and the whole-milk carton from the fridge. I'd fill the bowl—cereal bobbing in milk to the rim—and make my way to the parlor. There I'd turn on the television and begin what would be hours of watching my favorite cartoons. One cereal bowl would empty without my noticing, and I'd replace it. Bowl after bowl kept me busy as I sat cross-legged on the coffee table, which I'd move a secure twelve inches from the TV. Eating with eyes fixed on the TV was a hobby, something I learned to do as a way to occupy alone time.

Once Dad woke up, it was another two hours before he'd be

ready to start the day. So I'd play alone, making up a classroom or an elaborate game of house. I'd dress and re-dress my Barbies. I'd wash my Cabbage Patch Kids' hair and style it, an act that eventually led them to premature baldness.

The lightness, the playfulness Dad exhibited at night was absent in the morning and early afternoon. He was noticeably colder and more serious. He smiled as if it took something out of him. He joked less. Though I knew he'd just slept, he looked as though he'd just plodded in from the night shift. I knew he was never in the mood to talk before noon. I'd learned that one Christmas morning when he'd looked at me squarely and said, "I need a few cups of coffee before we can do presents." Mom tried to tease him, tried to get him to forego three mugs of black coffee with sugar, just so our excitement didn't fade by the time he was done with them. It was Christmas, after all, she reminded him. He looked at her hard. *Don't test me, Mere.* From the hunch of his shoulders and the way he had smoked slowly and methodically there in the living room, I knew how to treat him. Time and mood were always regulated by Dad. Our whole family was set to the thermostat, boiling or freezing, inside of him.

When he was ready—usually around four o'clock—he was willing to spend hours drawing whatever zany art project I dreamed up. We sketched—mostly underwater scenes. I found water fascinating, especially since I couldn't swim. I'd become afraid after nearly drowning on vacation in South Carolina. Dad had pulled me from the ocean floor, and I came up bubbling, spraying salt water from my mouth like a hose.

When we were done drawing, I'd decide to throw my picture away, because it was never as good as his. Not even close. I couldn't bear to see my illustration next to his, not when his was perfect. Later, when I was alone, I'd place his picture on the table beside me and strive to recreate it on a new sheet of construction paper. I wanted to make mine as good. I wanted Dad to like it. I got the sense that he loved whatever we did together just as much as I did. We crafted; we painted; we were wild. We even smashed eggs on the kitchen floor one afternoon when I told him I was angry. Mom wiped it all clean hours later.

In a way, his getting laid off from that job he loved meant I got all these endless afternoons and nights with him. I knew that it was a bad thing from the way he and Mom whispered about it. I didn't understand it in the same way that I didn't understand why I was bigger than my friends. Or why Anthony could catch a baseball with a glove and I could only catch it with my face. It was just the way things were.

Once school started, I was always late. Either Dad would have trouble getting up that morning, or we'd have trouble deciding on lime-green leggings versus purple leggings to go with the orange blouse he'd let me buy, a size too small, when Mom asked him to take me to Marshalls to get some clothes for school. When she later wanted to see my new outfits, I smiled and showed her a stack of paisley stationery, the orange blouse, two pairs of plastic dangly earrings, and one set of fake nails from CVS.

Other times we drove, just the two of us, in the family's two-door Toyota Tercel to pick up his unemployment check before school started. I remember those rides vividly. I can feel myself in that passenger seat, Dad veering close to the car parked to my right as he tossed a red-and-white Budweiser can casually onto the floor of the backseat. I looked out my window as our car swerved to narrowly slip past that parked car, and I remember clearly the silver of my seat belt sparkling in my periphery. It hung, loose and unused, on the door. I turned to the bag in my lap, hot with freshly fried Dunkin' Donuts. I picked up a cruller and bit into it, cracking the outer glaze into a yeast-risen center, and barely chewed before swallowing.

While Dad stayed home, close to a well-liquored fridge, Mom worked dawn into dusk, bleeding straight through weekends. I realize now that it would not be until her forty-eighth birthday that she would cut three jobs to two. I hated that she was gone. I despised every hour, every task she took on to keep us afloat. I knew she hated leaving at least doubly as much as I needed her to stay. The nights she'd work and I'd lie in bed with Dad, I'd cling to her pillow, my face planted in its plush center as I went to sleep. It wasn't her perfume or shampoo; it was that warm, milky scent of her skin alone, in the nook where her neck met her ear.

Some days she didn't have a day shift to follow her long night, and she would nap for three or four hours. She slept as little as her body allowed because she knew my morning routine in the parlor—the one with Care Bears and Pee-wee Herman and Cap'n Crunch. It was her motherly guilt, her intensely giving nature, I suppose, that rustled her from any stretch of deep sleep to join me.

She'd smile and kiss me, lingering, breathing into my curls, beaming to see her baby girl, even through exhausted, bleary eyes. She'd remind me that the coffee table wasn't a chair and that I needed to move away from the television set if I wanted to preserve my eyesight.

Most of the times when she was home during the day, she had a house that needed cleaning. For years, she made a steady but small income scrubbing and scouring stately homes in affluent neighborhoods near our home. I tagged along on almost all the two- or three-hour-long jobs when I was young. I suppose I could have stayed home with my toys, but I didn't mind spending a string of hours watching my favorite shows at whatever family's home needed disinfecting. And Mom, well, she just had to picture me spending a full day in the same pajamas, sitting on the coffee table in front of the TV, to make her mind up that toting me along with her cleaning supplies was more worthwhile than not.

I came to know the families who owned those homes. I'd sit, watching *Punky Brewster* in movie theater dimensions with surround sound. Mom would come into the room from time to time to again remind me that coffee tables weren't chairs, and I'd turn up the volume so as not to miss a word of my show. When she left, shaking her head, the stench of bleach and ammonia lingered in the room. Those chemicals and all the constant washing dried her hands so severely that they cracked.

When the housecleaning was over, I knew she'd keep her promise of driving through McDonald's. Mom was a woman of her word. Cheeseburgers with overly salted fries dipped in sweet ketchup were the reward for my patience, and for that, I was happy. But really, the meal meant more than lunch. She wasn't working; she wasn't cleaning our house or someone else's; she was there with me alone, eating in the car.

As we sat there in the drive-through line, delicious smells wafted into our open window. Grease and salt and beef seeped into the fabric of our seats. It hung in the air like a car freshener scented of deep fryer. Mom smiled as she leaned back to pass me my Happy Meal in a house-shaped cardboard box.

I grinned in anticipation. I took the box in my hands and then grabbed the vanilla milkshake I'd urged her to order despite both of us knowing I was going to drink her Coke, as well. I twisted open the rigid top of the box, and a puff of steam blew into my face. My right hand plunged deep inside to find what I cared about most: the cheeseburger. I tossed the toy on the floor, irritated that it had smooshed my bun.

In one of my favorite photographs, I see a terribly cranky three-year-old me sitting on Mom's lap. My mouth is smeared a deep cocoa brown, and my watery eyes reveal a recent crying fit. Mom is smiling as she hands me a Fudgsicle, and I am hushed. I see that the way my mother treated her babies was a cocktail of love and guilt. Half filled with sugary sweet love, topped off with the bitter guilt of having two children with a drunk father and an absent mother. The way she pacified me, the way she momentarily put that guilt to the back of her own mind, was by way of food. That girl version of me learned that I shouldn't experience discomfort. That whenever I start to feel even one inkling of boredom, doubt, anxiety, or anger, food would soothe me. At least temporarily. If I felt upset, Mom was able to distract me with the very mention of a treat. I'd forget whatever small act of terrorism I'd been committing in favor of cupcakes. She could trust the food to take care of me while she was away. She knew cereal sat with me while Dad slept, that McDonald's got me through a long and boring day of housecleaning, that she couldn't say no to any of my food requests when she knew full well how trying the rest of my girlhood would be. Food was a tangible thing that she could give when she couldn't give time and presence.

Just looking around at the food she made for birthday parties—the platters that would have made a supermarket look understocked—it was clear to everyone how Mom loved through food. "You really outdid yourself, Maryellen," they'd say as they shuffled out of the party at the end of the night. I didn't like it when they left. Family, friends, anyone—I wished they wouldn't leave us alone. Dad seemed especially on edge whenever we had guests over. During many of the parties that Mom threw, he'd be present for an hour at most, and then he'd retreat to the bedroom with a six-pack of beers in hand.

This night was no exception. When everyone had gone home, he came out to the kitchen. His eyes were only three-quarters open. Each blink was long and labored. A whiff of his breath smelled sweet turning sour. He walked through the rooms of our house in a purposeful yet clumsy way. As if he needed to get somewhere and he'd really like to be on his way, if only his feet would cooperate.

Mom turned to see him. She eyed him, but not in the same way she had before the party when he'd come into the kitchen in his underwear. When she realized I'd been watching her, she smiled at me. It reminded me of the smile she gave when she sat me down to tell me that Dad lost his job and that he'd get to spend more time at home with me. That was the kind of smile I didn't return. If smiles were as varied as the flavors of cupcakes, I'd found one I didn't like.

When he saw that the kitchen was filled with pots, pans, and dishes, Dad offered to help.

She took the porcelain gravy boat from his hands. "I've got it, Rob." I could tell she was using her polite voice. Ignoring her urges for him to go to bed and that she'd handle it, Dad moved around the kitchen picking up plates, shuffling them from one counter to the next, from the table to a chair, from the sink to the stove. I watched, puzzled, as he moved the dishes in no order closer to and farther from the sink. For a few minutes, Mom pressed her lips together to prevent impatience from spilling out of her mouth. I wondered if Mom would yell at him the way she yelled at me that time I spread Elmer's glue and flour on my bedside table playing bakery. "Rob . . . , please, honey." She reached for the stack of china that balanced on his forearms before he could take it to the living room.

"I'll clean up," he said and tried to move backward, angry at her interference.

Before she could take the plates fully into her own arms, he pulled his arms clean out from under them and the stack shattered beneath them on the tile. It felt as if minutes had passed before all the crashing and clanking stopped. Dad began yelling. "See what you did, Mere?!" When she began yelling back, I could see that her eyes were filling with tears. Instantly, mine filled, too. Those plates had been her favorite.

Dad's hollering sounded more like rumbling, like the earthquake that split the earth in *The Land Before Time*, when Littlefoot's mother died. His face puffed and reddened. Soon he was standing with his face so close to Mom's, I wasn't sure if his yelling would turn into a kiss, but she pushed him backward, and he stumbled toward the stove. "This is fucking bullshit!" he shouted. He tilted sideways to reach for his thick green glass ashtray on the kitchen table, and, before I knew what he needed it for, he cocked his arm back and swung it full force at the wall just to the left of where Mom stood. Mom shrieked, and that shrill sound, coupled with the smash of glass pummeling through plaster, made me yelp. I looked at the floor to find translucent shards of green glass all around Mom's feet. I noticed how closely they resembled the green apple Blow Pop I'd dropped on the sidewalk last weekend.

"Jesus, Rob!" Mom screamed, grabbing me and tucking my head into her chest. She held me as tightly as Anthony did when we wrestled. I felt the tears that raced down her cheeks splash onto my forehead, the tip-tops of my ears. Soon her tears were coming so fast, they slipped from her chin straight onto my eyelashes and halfway down my cheeks as if they were my own.

I stared as Dad stumbled backward and onto a chair at the kitchen table. Something had changed in him. The tiny red branches that sprouted in his eyes, the beads of sweat that poured from his temples—they frightened me. He no longer looked like my dad. He no longer looked like anyone's dad. Seeing him then was like staring at the old mahogany piano we had in our living room. When Mom brought it home from the antiques shop, I'd thought it was perfect, a unique treasure that was ours alone. But now that I'd been looking at it long enough, I could see its flaws: the grooves that ran like fault lines across the surface, how wobbly the whole thing was when it wasn't supported by the wall it leaned against, the nicks, the dings, the ways it had been damaged in a previous life and in ours.

By the following afternoon, all had returned to normal. Everyone went about living as if it were a typical morning, with no mention of the night before. Mom cleaned and swept the broken bits of ashtray into the trash; Anthony went to a friend's house to play flag football; Dad resumed his somber daytime routine. It seemed the only one who wasn't the same was me.

2

HE STARTED DRINKING MORE. I hadn't known it to be anything unusual until that Wednesday, at just about three o'clock in the afternoon, when I heard the glass shatter. If it had been just a smash—the crunch of another heavy green glass ashtray cracking through the wall—perhaps I wouldn't have flinched so markedly. If I hadn't heard Dad howl, I'd have assumed it was another routine case of him losing his temper.

At seven years old, I'd become accustomed to seeing ashes and cigarette butts flying through the air like confetti in the kitchen. They argued, usually after Mom pleaded with Dad to stop drinking or to help with some household task that might have made her life less overwhelming. Before she left for work, she'd ask for him to tidy up, and upon her return, she'd be met with a bigger mess. The dishes, in a crusty pile, waited to be bussed, and dirty laundry sat, almost patronizingly, just to the left of the hamper. She resented it. And he resented the nagging. Mostly, she backed down.

"Never mind. It's fine," she'd say, relenting. She took all the reasons she couldn't take it, not even a day longer, and packed them away. She rolled them, refolded them, and rearranged them, tucking them in and under and more tightly, as if she were filling a suitcase. Only patience made more room. She lugged that baggage with her, blistering the middles of her palms, and I could almost see the hunch her back had taken to support the weight. There were moments when she threatened him, said she wouldn't put up with all of it anymore. Those times, she'd stand straight up, her shoulders squared, with her suitcase at her feet, and I'd witness her body steel as it went from nervousness to self-assurance to hesitation to *just leave already!*

What I wonder now, when I think of how unbearably heavy that suitcase had become, how broken she looked every time she stuffed one more sorrow inside, is why she never left.

On the occasions when she chose to fight back, when she began unpacking the suitcase and setting its load upon Dad, his rage ignited. Even if he understood how valid her wants were, the attack made him defensive. He blasted her with her own insecurities over and over. The cursing, the name-calling, the insults—they corroded her confidence. They made her feel small. She ran our house and paid the bills by way of four jobs, and still I watched her weaken her stance and look downward as if to ask herself, *Is he right?* If she fought back, he roared louder. Or he'd throw something she loved across the room.

But those were not the times my chubby body trembled. Those weren't the times when my spirit split like the walls of our house. No, it was only when Anthony entered the room, when I heard his small voice try desperately to make itself bigger and less boyish, that the pit of my stomach twisted so violently, I couldn't tell if I was hungry or about to be sick. I'd see Anthony wedge himself between Mom and Dad, separating them by the width of his thin body. I'd watch him try his best to be brave, to speak through the staccato of his stutter. And at first, Dad would go easy on him. He'd gently tell him that everything was fine and that he should go back to his room. But with one look at Mom, Anthony planted his feet where they were. He stayed and tried to defuse the fight. Soon enough, Dad would begin launching insults at Anthony just as he'd done to Mom. The names he called him, the way he teased his fourteen-year-old son the way he might a man his own age—set the anger inside me over high heat. My insides rolled to a boil. I'd clench my jaw so tightly, I thought my teeth might crack.

I can still remember the last time I'd heard them fighting and Anthony had gotten involved. The three of them stood in the kitchen, and I looked on from the darkness of the dining room. My nails dug deeply into my palms when Dad began with the yelling. He belittled Anthony, taunted him, and then called him a faggot. My eyes darted around the room from Dad's red-hot face to Anthony's quivering bottom lip to Mom with one arm wrapped around her son and one arm outstretched toward her husband, keeping him at bay. I walked toward Dad with leaden legs. I bent slightly so that our eyes met—Dad seated in a kitchen chair that creaked under his 350 pounds, and me standing taller and twenty pounds heavier than any girl in my second-grade class. I felt as though my eyes were on fire. I moved my face to within inches from his, our noses nearly touching.

And then I told him that I hated him; that he was a bad, bad man, and I meant it. Mom drew my shoulders back, but I leaned farther into him as if to press my rage on him. I used words I hoped would cut into him in the same way I'd seen him cut Mom, cut Anthony, for the eight years I'd lived. I wasn't even sure at the time what my words would mean to him. In fact, I wasn't sure I even knew what I wished for him to be like, what I wanted out of a father. But then my thoughts rewound to episodes of *Full House* and *Little House on the Prairie,* where I came to know fathers like Danny Tanner and Pa Ingalls who were protectors and providers. And I was reminded briefly that my own was neither of those things.

When I finished hurling every angry thought I held at him, I searched Dad's eyes for recourse. I waited for him to do to me what he'd done to everyone else. I breathed hard, panting from adrenaline, into his face. I braced myself for whatever would come. He closed his eyes. My teeth gritted once more, as if tightening my face would harden my whole exterior into a shield. He opened his eyes, and the look he gave me wasn't anything I could have anticipated. What I saw in his eyes made my heart sink, made it deflate, just as it had two weeks earlier when the boys in my class called me fat while the girls looked on, smiling.

That day, my classmates had been running around the school yard at recess, laughing and whispering. I figured it was just boys being goofy about our second-grade teacher. It wasn't until one girl in my class—the one who had been teased for accidentally farting during gym class—approached me on the swings that I realized any of it had to do with me. She told me, as matter-of-factly as she'd once told me that I'd forgotten to return her pink mechanical pencil, that the boys wanted me to get off the swing set because they thought I was so fat that I'd break it. For a few seconds, I sat motionless, stunned. My face burned as I realized what she had just told me, and I looked around the playground, racking my brain for a joke, anything to say in return that would belie my embarrassment. And then I saw the group of them, all the boys and a handful of girls, standing on the pavement just under the basketball hoop, laughing at me. Laughing because of me. I turned my head down, tears welling and threatening to spill out and onto the peaches of my cheeks. I couldn't help but notice the way that the thin black rubber of the swing seat dug into the fleshy sides of my thighs. It reminded me of the way Mom tied up a pork roast, how the meat bulged between the thin white lines of string. I blinked a dozen times, hoping the flutter would fan the tears from my eyes. I couldn't bring myself to look back up. I feared she'd still be standing there, watching my humiliation. Worse, I feared she'd have one more mean thing to say.

The things I'd told Dad—they'd done what I'd intended for them to do. They cut him deeply. And when he turned his face away and picked up his beer can, upturning it into his mouth, I hated myself. I hated him for making me that angry. For teaching me that people listen when you yell louder, that you not only can cut them with your words, but you can pour hatred in their open wound. I hated Mom, even if I didn't realize it at the time, for letting me see his rage and then unleash my own. For letting me believe, even for a moment, that I had power, that I could be an adult in mind before body. I hated that in trying to stop the fighting, I'd waged a new war. And most of all, I hated that in trying to protect us all from the bully, to knock him down, I'd become one.

Mom said he never drank much before the year I was born. Six years after having my brother and marrying, Mom came home with a pink swaddled smoosh of wild black hair, full lips, and only a hint of a nose. And on January 25, my birthday, he fell down drunk. She cried, quietly and alone, with her face pressed into the nook of my little neck. She slept in Anthony's room that night, with me in the bed between them. In the morning, she opened her eyes to find Anthony smoothing my hair back on my head with his palm, whispering into my tiny ear. She smiled. "What are you telling your sister?" she whispered.

"That she can share my room with me."

The Wednesday when I heard the crash of glass in the hallway, I had been sitting in Anthony's room trying desperately to shove all of a wedding gown–bedecked Barbie into the front seat of her Corvette. It had taken almost an hour of convincing before Anthony caved and let me host the wedding there. I looked over at him, across the room playing *SEGA* on his TV. When I'd successfully managed stuffing the last bit of fabric into the car, I lay Ken across the trunk and pulled a caramel cream candy from the package in my lap. I untwisted the plastic wrapping and popped the whole thing into my mouth just as I heard the glass shatter.

I jumped as I bit down, my teeth squeezing through a glob of sticky caramel, and all the candies from my lap scattered about the floor. Dad cried out, "Mere!"

I heard her bare feet strike the few creaky floorboards as she ran to the breezeway.

Anthony hopped up instantly, calling a breathy "Andrea, come on" as he ran out through his bedroom door.

I sat motionless on the floor, listening to the commotion outside. I couldn't do anything but chew. I worked my way through the whole sticky center until it dissolved into gooey sugar on my tongue.

"Andreaaa! Come on!!" Anthony was shouting now.

They were already scurrying down the driveway, packing into our white Tercel as fast as they could. And I had to—simply had to—collect all my caramels. I urgently picked up each one that had scattered about the bedroom floor before getting up and rushing out of the room. I stuffed the candies deep within my pockets, the cellophane wrappers crackling as they settled into my denim overalls.

When I'd made it to the car, I could see that Dad was bleeding in the front seat. Anthony looked at him, so scared of the red seeping through the terrycloth towel wrapped around his arm. Mom was breathless and wide-eyed. She clenched the steering wheel and looked at me, standing outside the driver's window looking in.

I climbed in the back beside Anthony. He squeezed my pudgy fist and pulled it closer to his side.

Dad was furious. In between cursing at Mom and writhing in pain, he looked back to tell me and Anthony that he had cut his arm on the storm door. I nodded, knowing that any more questions would only make him angrier. By the time we pulled up to the emergency room, the once-yellow towel had been completely dyed red. Sopping and heavy with blood.

We sat in the waiting room while two nurses rushed Dad behind a set of large swinging doors. I wondered how they'd make his arm better—if he'd return with a big white cast like the kid in my class who broke his arm falling from the monkey bars. I tried to think of what I'd write on it and what color marker I'd use. After a while, a doctor came out from behind the doors and asked to have a word with Mom. They walked a few feet in front of where Anthony and I sat. And though Mom was using her quiet voice, I overheard her tell him that Dad had been drinking. They had been having a fight, and he accidentally punched his arm through a glass door. She swallowed before continuing that the glass had sliced open the whole length of his forearm, that from the way the blood gushed out, she thought he might have hit a vein, and . . .

I reached into my pocket for another caramel cream and unwrapped it, fumbling with the twisted plastic ends. The cellophane crackled so loudly, I couldn't hear the rest of what she said. Suddenly, I was starving—so hungry I couldn't get the candy into my mouth fast enough. The sound of my chewing was all that filled my head. Calm coursed through me.

I chewed each of my remaining caramels, one by one, until all that was left was a pile of shiny plastic wrappers on the seat beside me.

That day at the hospital was a turning point. Over the next few months, Mom stopped commenting on Dad's drinking. I no longer heard her plead with him to "take a night off" when the two of them were in the kitchen alone. She didn't stop him as he picked up the key ring and headed for the door after he realized the only drinks in the fridge were milk and Coke. She tells me now that she just didn't want to fight anymore. She tried to see if she could just put up with it, so that Anthony and I still had an intact family.

And so he drank.

The handful of nights when Mom didn't have a night shift, she cooked dinner, and we ate together. She'd make the most delicious meal, one of my favorites being meatloaf covered in a smoky-sweet glaze and served with potatoes she'd mashed with garlic, butter, and heavy cream. Those nights were the only ones when I didn't have to chew so loudly I couldn't hear what was going on around me. The plates, the napkins, the silverware—they all sat peacefully in place. We became more comfortable in our seats around the square butcher-block table. And lots of times we laughed as we ate meals as big as the whole of our four personalities. I'd feel, at least momentarily, that all was getting better. Dad would be his charming, brilliant self. He'd tell us stories that would make me laugh so hard milk went up my nose midgulp. Anthony's stutter would be less apparent. Each word, every sentence required less forethought when Dad didn't yell. It felt as if Dad had placed his foot on the one wobbly leg of our table, making it steady for once. And I'd begin to think that maybe we were becoming normal.

But there were times, perhaps midmeal, when something would rattle him—a sentence, a sound, anything at all—and almost instantly, Dad was done eating. It was as if he'd grown sick and tired of holding that table still, and he resented us for even asking him to keep his foot in place. Suddenly I'd feel my place setting shift slightly. I'd grab hold of my plate, sure that I could stop the sliding if I held tightly and acted as though the wobble didn't worry me. I'd work to keep the food on my plate sectioned securely. The peas had to maintain a strict border with the mashed potatoes, which couldn't dare touch the meatloaf. My buttered biscuit was quarantined. Having each food perfectly within in its own boundary made me feel calm. I'd take a bite from the potatoes and make sure to smooth them carefully back into place. I'd eat peas in rows so as not to disturb the line that stood between them and the meatloaf. And if the boundaries I had created on my plate broke—if those peas and potatoes mingled—I worked quickly to put them back into place.

The last meal I can remember eating together around the same table—all four of us—was in the early spring of 1994, the year I turned nine, just before Dad entered rehab and Mom told me we were moving. Dad's parents, Nana and Papa, decided to move permanently to the condo they owned in Myrtle Beach, South Carolina, rather than straddling the sunny South in winter and Medfield, Massachusetts, where they owned a house, in summer. Mom said that Nana and Papa eventually were going to give us their house and that, for now, we'd rent it from them. I didn't understand fully why we'd leave our home to live in a town fifty miles away. Anthony had just begun high school and pleaded for us to stay. My best friend, Lilly, told me to run away instead. But when I overheard Mom on the phone with her sister Maureen, I heard words like "foreclosure" and sounds of crying as she talked about not having enough money.

All eight of Mom's brothers and sisters drove up from Boston to Methuen that summer to help us move everything we owned to Nana and Papa's house in Medfield. I cried alone in my room. I found Mom crying, too, in our basement, just after everyone had left and we were readying ourselves for a final exit. I saw the way she bent over as she cried in the dark corner of the laundry room, trying to hide from Anthony and me so that we wouldn't know how much it killed her to leave. How badly she wanted to save our home for us, and how heavily failure weighed on her shoulders, and her heart, when she realized she couldn't. I watched her cry for ten minutes without letting her know I was there.

When school started that fall, I wanted nothing to do with it. I feared being not only the new kid but the fat one, too. The bell had already rung as I walked into Mrs. Harrington's fourth-grade classroom and made my way to the lone empty desk. I felt my cheeks flush as heads turned. I smiled at every person I passed with my mouth closed, since in first grade, kids had told me that the gap in my teeth and the chubbiness of my cheeks made me look like a chipmunk when I smiled wide. Half of me wished I hadn't come in late that first day so that I could have avoided such a pronounced entrance, while the other half wished I hadn't come at all. Seeing the way the other nine-year-olds looked at me made my pants feel tighter, made the waistband dig deeper into my belly. Everyone had moved on to wearing jeans, and I was still in stretch pants. Stir-rups, no less. I wore gold earrings when other girls had those cool stick-on holograms of stars and moons. I was out of place.

But a few months into the school year, I'd hit a kind of stride in Medfield. I learned that if I made fun of myself for being fat, then the other kids couldn't do it first. I learned that being funny, especially with the boys, made it much less likely they'd call me things like "wide load" and "lardbutt." I learned that certain jerseys in gym class were bigger than others and that I should always get to the pile of them first if I wanted mine to fit. I learned that even though the belts we wore while playing capture the flag never wrapped fully around my waist, they'd stay put if I tucked each end into my shorts. I learned that sometimes even your friends call you "whale" behind your back, but it doesn't mean they don't like you. I learned that it was easier to tell people that Dad was away on business rather than at home, drunk, and in his underwear. I learned that if I got invited to friends' houses after school, I'd probably be asked to stay for dinner, and that would mean not eating alone at home while Mom worked.

Just as soon as I began to adjust to our new life, I woke up to find Dad hadn't come home the previous night. Mom told me that he'd entered rehab. I sat at the kitchen table that morning, confused at the suddenness of his leaving. I came to learn, three days later from listening in on all Mom's phone calls, that the night he didn't come home, Dad had driven up the interstate while swigging from a gallon-size jug of vodka and had crashed into the guardrail on the right side of the road. He was en route to our old home in Methuen, where he had intended to park his car in the garage, close the door, and drink with the engine running until carbon monoxide filled the air enough to kill him. He hoped he wouldn't come back from that drive home. The day I pieced all of this together, I stayed home from school and ate five bowls of cereal in a row. I kept my eyes focused on the cereal box, the milk, and my bowl until all that was in the cabinet was gone. I ate until I felt so full, I couldn't move. Until I couldn't think of anything but the churning of my stomach as it digested Lucky Charms and Frosted Flakes and Trix.

The court took away his license. For two months the state held him in a rehabilitation facility three towns away from where we lived. When we visited him on weekends, he gave me art projects that he'd made during his free time—a painted ceramic Christmas ornament and a notebook of black-and-white sketches. He had us in stitches as he told stories about the various people he'd met in group therapy, using unique voices and gestures to mimic each. And when he finally came back to us, he seemed a stable man. He rode his bicycle around Medfield. He got a paper route. He helped me with my homework, and we played video games for hours on end—while Mom found a third and fourth job, trying desperately to make ends meet. From the way she seemed panic stricken all the time, I should have known that things weren't going well. I should have known that something was wrong when I tagged along with her on our weekly Sunday grocery shopping trips, and she told me our budget was twenty-five dollars. But somehow I still felt blindsided by the news that we had to leave our new home. Nana and Papa had lost patience with Dad, with our missing rent for a few months, and two weeks before Christmas 1994, they told Mom we had to leave their house by the first of January. There was no negotiating, no convincing them, even when Mom pleaded with Nana, "But, Kay . . . , we've got nowhere to go. Please." We packed all our belongings in trash bags and liquor store boxes and moved into a two-bedroom apartment in Wilkins Glen, Medfield's low-income housing, by the start of 1995. The second of January, unbeknownst to us, my grandparents changed the locks and trashed all our remaining possessions there.

Three weeks later, just after my tenth birthday, Mom signed me up for a bowling league. All my new friends had joined. Thursday afternoons after bowling, the bus dropped us off in front of the school, and I'd look out the frosted window to see the usual caravan of Caravans. Parents lined up to greet us. With a quick scan, I knew which parent belonged to which kid—and that in the whole crowd, no one was searching for me.

Most weeks I'd catch a ride from someone, saving me from a two-mile walk home. One of the parents would be kind enough to shuttle me, even though I lived farther away than they'd like. No one ever said it, but I sensed the silent sigh in the "Sure!" I noticed the brief flinch as we bounced over the speed bumps leading into my apartment complex. They'd smile into the rearview mirror as they remarked, "How nice they keep the grounds around here!" I'd smile back, feeling momentarily lucky that the low-income housing we moved into at least looked respectable.

One particular Thursday, I hopped off the last step of the bus and saw Dad there. He'd stopped drinking and had taken to riding his bike again. I noticed how cold the air was that hit me. The temperature bent as low as New England weather knew to limbo. He was wearing a puffy down jacket, so loud in color that I could practically hear it shout "I'm royal BLUE!!" Snug on his head was a ski cap that some company must have been giving out as promotional swag at a conference years ago, when he held a job. It was obnoxious in its green, tan, and mustard glory. Brown, deconstructed. A pom-pom made of cheap yarn flailed from its top.

I gasped at the sight of him. Worse than his clothing was the old mountain bike. I was certain that it had rotted for years in someone's garage before it finally hit the lawn of a yard sale.

"What are you doing here?" I said.

He smiled. He must have assumed that as a kid who rarely had a parent to pick her up, I would be thrilled. Instead, I was aghast. If *horrified* had a "Which emotion am I?" poster in a psychologist's office, it was my face.

He had come to pick me up. To ride along beside me as I walked home from school. I waved to my friends and their parents, letting them know I didn't need a ride, and began the walk. He followed, keeping up with my chubby-legged superstride. I asked him to "Please, please, please, please, take off your hat."

"Wha—no! Why? It's cold out."

"It's so ugly and I hate it and . . . you're embarrassing me."

I paused and then said, "I want you to go away."

"Andrea, c'mon. That's crazy talk." He offered a sheepish smile, continuing to pedal.

Adamant now, I stopped. He braked as I turned to face him. "I don't want anyone to see me with you. I don't want you to ride beside me."

And with that, his eyes changed. I could see I'd wounded him. His mouth hung slightly open, as if he had one last plea in him, *but, oh, never mind.*

I walked away from him, heading right as he steered slowly left. I didn't turn around. I felt so sure of myself in that moment, so positive that I was making a necessary decision. I believed that avoiding embarrassment, all the dreamed-up humiliation in my head, was worth pushing away a dad who came to pick me up from school.

An hour later I'd made it home and was unable to acknowledge the shame, the guilt, of what had happened earlier.

I lingered in the doorway of the kitchen, spilling a cereal supper, and looked at him, seated at the dining room table. He looked back at me and I could see that he'd had a drink when he had gotten home. His eyes looked cloudy and glazed. I wondered if what I'd done had made him veer his bicycle up North Street to the liquor store.

He turned back to the table, and I looked down at my floating Apple Jacks—milk logged and bloated. "I'm sorry," I mouthed, so quietly that no one could hear.

I thought briefly to sit with him, but I walked to the den instead, face downturned to my bowl, tears salting the peach-hued milk.

For months he continued to drink in the same reckless way he always had. Then spring came, and he went missing.

Two full days passed before the phone rang and Mom rushed to the kitchen to answer it, while I ran to the one in the living room to catch it, somehow both of us knowing it would be him.

"Mere," he began, his voice unsteady.

She stretched the coiled phone cord from the kitchen wall all the way down the hallway and leaned into the living room where I was. With her hand over the receiver, she told me to hang up. Her eyes warned me against protesting. I placed the cordless phone back in its base, and she hurried out of the room.

Impatient, I lasted one minute waiting in the living room before racing down the hallway. By the time I reached her, she was off the phone. She told me to get my coat, that we were going to get Dad.

I pressed her for details, and she gave me a desperate look. Her eyes scared me. They darted around the room frantically, as if looking for Anthony, who was out with his friends. "Francie, Dad . . . tried to kill himself." Her words rolled out like an apology. He had checked into a motel by the highway, where he swallowed a full bottle of pills and drank a handle of vodka.

Dad entered Tewksbury State Hospital. In the weeks that followed, he underwent intensive group and individual therapy. He was sober for twenty-eight days straight. When he returned home, he told us he'd met a guy in the hospital who became a friend. That friend had a place out west, in Arizona. Dad was sure he could go to the desert, stay with his friend, stay clean, and then come back to us a new person. He said he just needed to get away for a while. He'd come back—he promised—just as soon as he got his feet on the ground again.

In June he took a train westward with nothing but a box of Saltine crackers and called us from Phoenix three weeks later. We heard in his voice that he had been drinking. His sentences were choppy and nonsensical. He asked Mom to send him money to take the three-day train back home. And when she did, he came back to us.

For one full year, from that summer of 1995 straight through the following spring of 1996, Dad kept leaving for and returning from Arizona. Every month or so, I'd hear Mom on the phone with him, agreeing to send him whatever money we had. Each time he returned to us, he'd inevitably find that staying sober in Medfield was worse than drinking alone in the desert. He convinced Anthony to apply to Arizona State University, saying that the Southwest was going to be a great place for the two of them. And despite Mom's pleas and tears, Anthony went with him in the fall. I hated that part of the country, if only for the reason that it had lured them both away. I realized that their leaving took Mom away, too—to work. I kept the televisions on in every room of our empty apartment to combat the loneliness that comes with silence.

When the next June came, and I was a blink from finishing sixth grade, Dad called. I knew from Anthony, who saw less and less of him the longer he was there, that Dad was drinking heavily. I even knew that Dad had, on more than one occasion, drunkenly humiliated Anthony in front of his friends.

And now he needed money again. He needed to come home, I heard him tell her over the phone. She didn't have a dime. Part of her knew that it was best for Anthony, who had decided to take a semester off from school, and me that we not live with an alcoholic, albeit our dad. The other part of her loved him fiercely and wanted him home, safe and sound regardless of sobriety. She also remembered the three previous times she'd sent him that same money.

"Rob, I'm sorry, I can't."

With that, she passed me the phone. My heart raced, not knowing whether to support her decision and act like a grown-up, or to tell him that I missed him and wanted him home, which was the truth. He asked me to convince Mom to send him money. He told me how much he wanted to come home, how different things would be this time.

"But Dad, you never change . . . you never get better. Mom's right." I choked on my own words. "You shouldn't come home."

And through the spiral telephone cord, I felt his eyes close. A nod. I heard what he didn't say: *I can't believe you said that, Andrea. I hate you for saying that, Andrea. But . . . I know. I know.* And as I told him I had to go, I felt my throat close up. I felt as though I'd swallowed my heart.

On Sunday, November 23, 1997, the night before I was supposed to have read all of Dickens's *A Christmas Carol* for English class, the phone rang. I sat on the edge of Mom's bed as she picked up her bedroom phone.

She turned to face the wall, and I stared down at Dickens. I heard the phone click back in the receiver.

I looked up at her, ready to tell her that I hated reading and Dickens and seventh grade, but her eyes stopped me. They said it before her mouth could. "Dad's dead."

I ran to my room and sobbed into the clothes hanging in my closet. I hated the feeling of the fabric against my face. I wanted to tear all the clothing from its hangers. I hated my First Communion dress and how roughly the coarse white material rubbed against my wet cheek. I hated Mom for wanting me to save it, since she'd had a wedding dress cut down to fit me. I hated that since the dress was a women's size twelve, she thought I could probably wear it again when I grew up. I knew how impossible that was—and how no one wears their First Communion dress again after second grade. I thought of how everyone just gets bigger as they grow up. And then I hated that, too.

When I search frantically through my memories of the rest of that night, I can only hear two sentences: the ones Mom said to Anthony and me in her bedroom. "Dad died last July in Arizona. He had a stroke, and they found him at the train station."

I scan the days that followed. I remember odd bits and pieces of the time, little snippets of phone calls, my brother's face, the hunch of my mother's heaving back as she lay in bed facing the window the next morning. That time is like a scratched CD, the song coming in and out of lyrics and harmonies. Fragments of melody at best. The whole month of November 1997 is jagged and disjointed and holey.

But I clearly remember the food. I remember the J.J. Nissen blueberry muffins that my Nana brought that Monday morning. The way the moist muffin top sort of gelled to my fingertips. How I finished two and smashed the empty wrappers between two cupped palms on my way to the trash can. I remember the creaminess of 2% milk and the tart zing of ice-cold Newman's Own Lemonade. I can't remember the exact conversations, the dress I wore to his funeral, what my brother said in his eighteen-year-old's eulogy, what I told my seventh-grade friends when they called and asked if I could do a part of some project for class on Wednesday. I can't remember crying more than twice.

All I can think of is the gummy crumbs of a store-bought blueberry muffin. The oversize rings of oil that bled through the white parchment-paper muffin liner. Thanking my Nana and Aunt Margie for bringing us a haul of groceries.

The way I swallowed then, when I needed anything but to feel, was precarious. Desperation and regret. A sharp gulp. A jagged clump of blueberry muffin in that space between my tonsils, working its way down to rest in my belly. It's hard to tell if it's a knot of tears welling in my throat, or a hunk of food that has barely been chewed before being swallowed. The knot sinking lower and lower, like a tennis ball being pushed through panty hose.

I'd eat this way, hard and purposeful, all the days following his death. I found momentary relief in discomfort of another sort. In feeling as if my stomach could sate that hole where a dad, alcoholic or not, used to be. The muffins, those bloated Apple Jacks—I pushed them forcefully into my mouth with the hope that they would distract me.

But they did not.

They could not.

I ate as ragefully as I felt. I swallowed uncomfortably. I kept my head bent and hanging, to my bowl, shamefully. I filled myself desperately.

Food numbed me.

I wish I remembered his face as precisely as I remember eating the muffins, one after another, the morning after Mom told me he'd died. I wish I hadn't found out that the reason we didn't know where Dad was for five months, two weeks, five days, and nine hours—since I'd told him not to come home—was because he was homeless and without any form of identification on him. I wish he'd had more than two pennies in his left pocket. I wish he hadn't been sleeping in a boxcar in the scorching desert heat, after drinking himself into oblivion. I wish they hadn't had to identify him by his teeth, and that they hadn't just put him in a simple pine box and misplaced his file, forgetting to call his next of kin until November.

I wish I had a better photograph in mind when I think of him now than the one the coroner sent us to verify that the body they found, homeless and alone, was, indeed, Robert F. Mitchell. I wish his eyes had been closed in that picture, or even cloudy and sweet with booze again. Anything but scared and cold and gone.

When I wanted to forget that picture of my broken father, I ate. I hung sweet and savory pictures over the ones that haunted me. I framed the food instead.

3

I LEARNED TWO VERY IMPORTANT THINGS in the wake of Dad's death. One was that losing him meant I could also temporarily remove the name tag I'd worn for years that read "the fat girl" and replace it with something more compassionate: "the girl whose dad died." Kids passing me in the hall would offer a look that said *I'm sorry, and not just because I laughed when they called you a wide load on the bus last week*. I'd return a silent thank-you and realize that none of it mattered anyway.

The second thing I learned was that school was the only place where I wasn't alone. And I began to love it for that reason. I began to crave it.

The sadness I felt then, and even sometimes now, blares within me. It's an all-encompassing, piercing sound—a fire alarm. It shrieks so loudly, I cower. I seek refuge by covering my ears. I think briefly about ducking beneath a stairwell, hoping its shrillness will be muffled if I hide from it. But it finds me, always. It finds me when I'm in the shower or walking on a treadmill; it wakes me suddenly in the night. It forces me to uncover my ears. And I hear it while trying not to listen to what it means. The pain, the sound—it's deafening. After listening for so long, I become immune to it. The urgent alarm turns to a hollow ringing, a monotone that feels far away and permanent. And sometimes, though the dull pain in my ears reminds me, I can make myself forget I'm hearing it at all.

Eating made me forget. The flavors, the textures, and smells entertained me enough to mute my other senses. Filling my belly stuffed my mind so completely that no space existed for sadness. Packing myself with sweets until I ached created a new sensation, one that had nothing to do with intense loneliness and broken dads.

The kitchen, too, made me forget. That galley in our apartment had become the only space at home I could tolerate. The cramped quarters felt comforting. Staying in there prevented me from lingering in the vulnerability, the wide-openness of reality.

In hindsight, I see so clearly the isolation, the desperation for attention and affection of any kind that absorbed me. Mom returned to work three days after the funeral. Anthony didn't go back to school in Arizona. He began staying out with friends all night, working, doing anything to avoid coming home. I was desperate for one of them to stay with me, to keep me from feeling as though Dad's death was eating away at me, slowly and alone. But neither ever did. And I never asked them to.

I prayed for invitations to hang out with friends, for anything that might involve a real plated meal and a family. Our home had become the loneliest place I'd ever been, and I hated it. I hated that I was the one who had to lock the front and back doors to our apartment each night before heading to bed. I hated worrying that another tow truck might show up early in the morning to repossess our car and that maybe this time I'd be the only one home. I hated worrying that the electric company might turn off the lights again, and then I'd be left not only alone, but in darkness, too. I hated myself for wishing that Anthony felt guilty for going out, because I understood why no one would want to remain in our lifeless home. I hated the feeling of helplessness, of knowing that Mom was working to support me while I sat at home gorging myself on almost all of the only food she could afford. I hated it each time I stuffed the cardboard of a cereal box into our trash can, knowing that I'd just eaten five bowls and she'd eaten none.

But hating it didn't change anything; it didn't fill our home with more people, more food, or more comfort. None of us could offer each other anything substantial. Not Mom, not Anthony, not me. Instead, Mom and Anthony left, surviving by busying themselves. And I, for my part, ate.

When I'd finish eating all the sweets in our kitchen, usually a measly three days after Mom had gone grocery shopping, I'd begin baking. I restocked our cabinets with homemade treats. Almost exclusively, I lifted recipes from the pages of the one, the only recipe book that sat on our counter: *The Silver Palate Cookbook,* our favorite. Mom, concerned with even the mention of clutter, wasn't the kind to leave things out—especially things that belonged on bookcases or in cabinets. That she let that tome keep company with her KitchenAid stand mixer on the counter meant something.

Since my fifth birthday, I had been Mom's apprentice every time she baked. I shadowed her as she beat butter and sugar into glossy gold batter for bishop's cake. We made luscious lemon squares with tart, bright notes of citrus and a buttery shortbread base. She let me dust powdered sugar across their gooey tops. I helped by cracking eggs into the bowl and running a knife along the top of her measuring cups, letting the excess flour drop off the sides. I learned the timing. I learned the precision. I learned the delicate nature of baking. And my favorite: the requisite taste testing. There was value in licking every battered spoon and every frosting-laden finger. What, exactly, that value was, I'm not aware, but my belly knew, and I'd say that's enough. I left most major decisions to that part of me—to the wisdom of my waist.

Having spent years at Mom's side, asking questions, watching cupcakes dome through the oven door, I learned to read almost exclusively by recipe cards. They served as flash cards, lined up neatly in the pattern of the alphabet. *Apple Pie, Banana Bread, Carrot Cake* . . . And somehow, without consciously realizing the transition, I became the baker. I sat there in our kitchen—now thirteen and unsure if it was hunger or just loneliness that brought me there—and recreated the confections we once made together. The ones that drew me, nose first, into the kitchen tied themselves to moments in my life and tucked themselves away in the closet of my memory.

Double fudge brownies as fat and dense as bricks, coconut white-chocolate blondies, cashmere custards so thick they'd remain stuck to a spoon held upside down, spicy molasses cookies, and all things that conjured lust. As I yanked each of them from the oven's mouth, never quite making a clean getaway without some form of heat blister, I felt full. Our apartment wasn't so lonely with two dozen cupcakes cooling on the kitchen counter. It wasn't so quiet when the timer dinged and the mixer churned. There was less to notice when my hands were knuckle-deep in kneading dough.

And when I wasn't baking, when I wasn't all alone in my own

kitchen, Mom drove me to Boston to stay with her sister Maureen; Maureen's husband, Mike; and their kids, Michael, Matt, and Meredith. I spent weekends, summer breaks, vacations, and holidays with them when Mom had to work. If only I'd had an *M* name, I might have forgotten that I wasn't one of them. Maureen and Mike treated me no differently than their own children; my cousins—all around my age—accepted me as a sister. I experienced a kind of nurturing—a sense of structure and normalcy—that I hadn't known before. I was happy there. I was a kid there. But sometimes, in quiet moments when I'd turn the corner into their kitchen to see Mike tinkering with a school project for Michael, or when I'd take notice of Matt's report card hung proudly on the fridge, or when I'd watch Maureen French-braid Meredith's hair for her dance recital, I'd be jolted back to the reality that this perfect family was not truly mine. At my house, no one was there to help me with projects, no one knew if I brought my report card home or not, and even if Mom could braid my hair, it would be unlikely that she'd be able to make it to my recital. When Mom would come to pick me up, even though I'd have missed her terribly, I'd stare out the car window as we'd drive away, back toward Maureen's big, beautiful yellow house and wish that I could stay.

Back in Medfield, I found other surrogate families—those of my best friends, Kate and Nicole. Nicole's dad, Paul, was the one to drive me home most school nights after he'd cooked dinner for all of us. I always felt a pang of guilt, no matter how many times he reassured me that it was no trouble at all shuttling me back to my apartment, because I knew it couldn't have been easy to juggle all that he did. On top of being a volunteer firefighter, he also worked a full-time rotating shift—nights and days—as a gas control operator. I hadn't known many men to work so tirelessly. I hadn't known even one, in fact, who not only went to work at multiple jobs but also helped to clean the house, cooked dinner, and would still be present for every Youth Soccer game his three daughters had. The seasons that I played in that soccer league, Mom only made it to one game. But Paul was there, on the sidelines at every game, running down the field and cheering for me as I dribbled the ball—just as he did for Nicole.

Perhaps because of the baking, perhaps because of Paul's unbelievable spaghetti and meatballs, surely because of the way I ate, I gained twenty-five pounds during seventh grade, bringing me to two hundred pounds total. And though I had only ever grown outward, Mom hadn't made me aware that she noticed. In fact, Mom was the only one, other than Anthony, who never acknowledged my size. I look back in amazement that Anthony had never once hurled the word *fat* at me as an insult the way my classmates had. Not many people in my family did, except Dad's mom, Nana. She was the one who had been microwaving Lean Cuisines for me all the years I could remember.

Each summer, when Anthony and I stayed with her and Papa in South Carolina for the month of August, Nana made sure to stock up on food for our stay. On her counter sat a box of twelve sticky cinnamon-pecan buns glazed so thickly with white frosting, you could barely see their coiled centers—and they were all for Anthony. Next to them, for me, sat a package of sugar-free, fat-free Jell-O pudding cups—and not even the ones with the vanilla in the middle. The freezer, too, was split between Anthony's food and mine. He had the Klondike bars, I had the Lean Cuisines, and we all had the tray of lasagna that she'd made a decade before, give or take a year. In the mornings, Nana suggested I sprinkle Equal on my Rice Krispies so that I could "keep my sugar down," just like she did, to manage her diabetes. Still concerned, she sat me down one afternoon to tell me that she was disturbed by how many bananas I'd eaten. I hadn't even realized one could eat too many bananas, let alone be concerned about it. I looked at Nana and nodded, ashamed of my fruit consumption. But as she started to get up, I noticed the trouble. She was stuck within the arms of the chair. At five feet two inches tall, Nana weighed well over three hundred pounds. Her belly—like Dad's—preceded her. Perhaps she didn't want me to end up as she had. Perhaps she thought she could fix me. But all I gathered from her actions and suggestions was that fat people should eat diet food, while skinny people could eat delicious food.

Mom wasn't like that. She never even brought a scale into our home. For better or worse, she let numbers and measurements live in doctors' offices and in the mall beside the bathroom where people could pay twenty-five cents for an unpleasant reality check.

Instead, she rubbed my back when people in school began to tease me more. When I came home and cried after being humiliated in homeroom, she supported me rather than suggested I change. My weight was something that we both wished were different, but neither of us spoke of it as something fixable. We treated my fat in the same way we treated New England winters: wishing they weren't so burdensome, but accepting that they probably wouldn't change anytime soon.

It wasn't until my annual physical in eighth grade, just after I turned fourteen, that Mom and I began to think differently about my weight. We sat in the doctor's office, just as we'd done year after year, waiting for my doctor to comment on how big I was before letting us go. This time, though, he breathed deeply and then held my growth chart in front of him for us to see. I looked at the graph, marveling at the line that rose steadily upward and to the right, from 1985 until that day in 1999. He traced a finger along the line, explaining that my weight since birth had increased rapidly, and that the rate at which I was still gaining was alarming, to say the least. He paused. "Andrea, my girl, you've got to lose weight." What he said next has always stuck with me: "At this rate, I predict you'll weigh three hundred pounds by the time you turn twenty-five." As if in sync, my stomach and jaw dropped. My heart stopped beating for a solid ten seconds. Mom reached over to hold my hand. I was horrified. So horrified that big fat tears came rolling down my cheeks as he rattled off a list of suggestions to help me lose weight. "Eat more fruit, try whole wheat bread, don't eat cookies..." I stopped listening after the one about joining a sports team for exercise, too scared to even feign interest.

To say I was overwhelmed in that moment would be as much of an understatement as saying I was a little pudgy. When my doctor left and closed the door behind him, Mom grabbed my face in her hands, looked into my saltwatery eyes, and assured me: "Francie, now you listen to me. You're the most beautiful being I've ever laid eyes upon." And though every mother might spout the same sentiments, I knew mine wanted nothing as much as she wanted me to believe her words.

We left the office, and I cried all the way to lunch at Pizzeria Uno, where we sat in a leather booth built for two and talked earnestly for the first time about losing weight. I felt vulnerable acknowledging with Mom how big I'd gotten, when weight had always kept a quiet and immutable existence. I didn't say it aloud, but I recognized the oddity of talking about eating healthier while swigging a Sprite, just one of the many things the doctor suggested that I eliminate from my diet. I picked french fries from my platter of chicken fingers and brought them to my mouth quickly, compulsively, as though clearing my plate were the first order of business in making room for change. I finished my meal and even helped with some of Mom's, and what I was left with was an odd tug-of-war between hating and pitying myself. I could feel the fat clinging tightly to me as it always had, and now, at the very thought of having to rid myself of it, I felt it cling tighter. At fourteen and two hundred pounds, I couldn't help but feel burdened by my weight. Worse, I was saddled with the fact that I was the one who had to actively lose it.

I thought of my best friends, how they ate, and how I seemed to eat no differently. After school, we all ate the same Drake's chocolate cakes with cream filling. We all stirred chocolate syrup into our milk. We all knew which houses handed out full-size candy bars on Halloween. I believed that my body had betrayed me. Unwilling to accept any responsibility, I thought I'd been unfairly stuck with fat for no reason.

Within a week, I grudgingly began my first diet. Mom had read an advertisement for a voluntary clinical weight loss study being conducted on young women at Brigham and Women's Hospital in Boston. She came home with a stack of forms she'd already filled out and signed. "It's a good opportunity for you," she promised, her voice soothing and hopeful. She explained that I'd learn a great deal, that I'd have a support system. And though I couldn't muster enthusiasm or even a shred of confidence, I wanted badly to believe her.

The study aimed to observe the effects of a new and experimental weight loss medication called Meridia (sibutramine). The drug was an appetite suppressant whose desired effect was reduction of hunger and, in turn, food consumption, thereby encouraging weight loss. This exact medication type has since been withdrawn from the US market by the Food and Drug Administration (FDA) and in several other countries for its potentially dangerous side effects.

Half of the group of twenty volunteer girls, ages twelve to seventeen, would be administered the drug itself; the other half would be taking a placebo. Neither group would know which pill they took: real or fake. Over the course of three months, the girls would meet every other week to be weighed and measured and to talk collectively with a team of registered dietitians.

At first, it seemed like a reasonable idea. At our first Saturday-morning group meeting, I met ten girls, each seated next to her mother, and our lead nutritionists. I scanned the room when we all sat down and immediately noted our similarities. We were all big, all squished into chairs with thin metal arms that dug into our thighs, all fidgeting and uncomfortable, all clearly wishing we were somewhere—anywhere—else. I looked around at each of the mothers and noted that none of them was thin. Like their daughters, each carried at least twenty extra pounds. I wondered if they hoped to lose as much weight as they wanted their daughters to lose by enrolling them in this study. I looked to our main nutritionist as she tugged at her gauzy muumuu, readjusting it so that it draped over her belly like a towel over a beach ball. *How can she be fat?* I wondered.

Just as I began to dive into the impossibility of a fat woman guiding me to thinness, the meeting began. In the first ten minutes, we introduced ourselves and our mothers. Then we moved on to what the mission of our group would be: to support each other while learning to eat well and move more. It was encouraging to feel connected and on the same path, but I felt embarrassed to have to be part of it.

Daily, outside of meetings, each of us girls was to take the prescribed dose of Meridia or the placebo and do our best to follow a set of healthy eating and exercise guidelines not unlike the food-guide pyramid prescribed by the FDA. The main guidelines, as I remember them now, included suggestions such as:

1. Drink eight 8-ounce glasses of water per day.
2. Eat five or more servings of fruits and vegetables per day.
3. Switch all white flour/refined-grain products to those made entirely with whole grains.
4. Limit sweet foods composed mostly of sugar (cakes, cookies, pastries).
5. Move your body for thirty minutes per day (walking, jogging, dancing, swimming).

After two weeks of diligence, my heart sank as I weighed in, having lost only half a pound. I forged on for another two weeks and when the nurse told me privately that I had gained a pound, I cried alone in the bathroom stall before our group meeting. I had failed. I could almost feel the pound of fat I'd gained, hanging low on my belly, next to all the rest, and I hated myself for it.

Reflecting now on the way I ate during the first two weeks of the study, I recognize the errors. The foods I learned to be healthy—the foods that are indeed healthy in proper portions—I munched with abandon. A cupped handful of almonds, which I thought to be a light snack, tacked five hundred calories onto my daily intake. The yogurt I asked Mom to buy was the kind that came sweetened and topped with crushed Oreo cookies. The Honey Bunches of Oats cereal that I was certain qualified as health food wasn't quite so virtuous three bowls in.

While the dietitians at our group meetings introduced me to a world of healthy food—even going so far as to take us on a field trip to Whole Foods to marvel at the rainbow of produce—they must have forgotten to mention portion sizes. Knowing all that I know now about nutrition, I see how easy it was for me to fail at this diet. As a girl who always ate self-determined, larger-than-large servings of whatever I wanted, I needed to learn that most things in life, like cereal and orange juice, shouldn't be bottomless. Because few foods are healthy when eaten in third and fourth helpings. Calories should have been part of the conversation we had in those group meetings. Not to make us obsessive counters, but to make us aware that food has value and that too much of anything costs us something nutritionally.

By nightfall, I'd secretly eaten three packages of Little Debbie Swiss Cake Rolls. I plunged the empty wrappers deep into the trash can, below a wad of paper towels so that Mom wouldn't find them and become as disappointed in me as I already was with myself. If she noticed the missing boxes, she never said anything. In the week that followed, I put in a halfhearted healthy effort. I craved all things sweet so intensely that I continued to eat them, lots of them, in secret. Guilt and Oreos sat heavy in my stomach.

I wanted badly to be smaller, to be less painfully aware of my size, but I just wasn't ready to stick to an apple when cookies were the afternoon snack my friends enjoyed. I didn't feel like moving more. It wasn't fair that I needed to exercise when my best friends simply walked around the mall en route from Orange Julius to Auntie Anne's Pretzels. I resented having to live differently just so I could be the same.

My best friend, Kate, was a bodily enigma. All her life she'd been very, very thin—a lean and bony waif in all the pictures I'd ever seen of her from birth through adolescence. With her long blond hair, she looked like Gwyneth Paltrow—beautiful and delicate. The way she ate seemed no different from the way I ate. If we spent a Saturday together, fresh off a Friday night sleepover, here is how our eating played out: In the morning we'd sit at her kitchen table, and Kate would place two bowls, two spoons, a jug of 1% milk, and the box of Honey Bunches of Oats with Almonds in front of us. The very acknowledgment that Kate adored cereal as much as I did, and that she ate it every morning, was enough to tell me that there was nothing wrong with how much I craved it. In turn, I assumed cereal wasn't anything to avoid and that my eating it was perfectly fine.

But setting the whole box on the table was contrary to what I'd learned in group. They'd told us we should serve ourselves from the kitchen, take our plate to the table, and eat. If we were still hungry, we could go back for more. The dietitians explained that having the full box there led to mindless overconsumption, that we'd probably serve ourselves more just because it was there. Kate and I poured equal amounts of cereal into our bowls, about a cup and a half. We splashed milk on top just to cover the flakes. And then we ate, chitchatting through the crunchy bites. What I didn't recognize then—what I failed to notice—was that Kate stopped after one bowl of cereal. She ate so slowly that I was able to fill a second bowlful by the time she'd made it halfway through her first.

When lunchtime came, we convinced Kate's mom to take us to Taco Bell. There, Kate would order two crunchy tacos with "beef and cheese only, please," while I got two Beef Supreme Chalupas. The only difference for our orders, we both acknowledged, was that Kate disliked sour cream, zesty sauces, and soft taco shells. A mere matter of preference, I was sure. And though each of us had ordered two, I now know that Kate's tacos clocked in at 170 calories each, while mine were a whopping 370 calories each.

Late in the afternoon, back at Kate's house, after we'd tired of creating binder collages of Leonardo DiCaprio and watching recorded episodes of *The Real World: Seattle*, we'd head into her kitchen for a snack. She always had Pepperidge Farm Milano cookies, and for that, I worshipped her cupboard. Kate pulled two from the package, set them on a napkin, and ate them as slowly as she'd eaten breakfast. I pulled out two at first, but when I finished and noticed she still had one left to eat, I reached into the bag for two more.

As dinner approached, Mom would come and pick Kate and me up from Kate's house and take us to dinner and a movie, a tradition we held on Saturday nights. Pizzeria Uno was almost always the chosen spot. There Kate ordered the chicken fingers and french fries from the kids' menu while Mom and I ordered the same thing in adult versions. Each of us cleared our plates, Mom paid the bill, and then we'd run into a convenience store near the movie theater to grab sodas and candy bars for the show. Kate got a package of Reese's, and I did, too, along with a Kit Kat. We'd each grab a twenty-ounce Coke from the cold case, and at the end of the movie, Kate would still have a nearly full bottle. Her stomach was so tiny, she couldn't drink as much as I could, I reasoned.

After the movie, Mom dropped Kate off, and we returned

home. What I know now about those nights was that Kate went straight to bed, while I grabbed an assortment of Little Debbie and Hostess cakes and sat down for an hour of television before hitting the sack.

A few weeks into the group study, after weight loss had eluded me weigh-in after weigh-in, I convinced myself that I was in the placebo group. I stopped taking the prescribed pills. I was sure that no improvement to my appetite was being made by taking them anyhow. Mom urged me to continue, thinking that something was better than nothing, but I resisted. And though I didn't say it aloud, I began to resent her for the mixed messages she sent me. I resented her wanting me to lose weight while telling me that I was perfect the way I was. I resented that she encouraged me to eat better but still agreed to drive me through Burger King for a Whopper Meal if I asked her. I resented not only that I began sneaking into the kitchen to eat Oatmeal Creme Pies in secret, but that she bought them, along with Yodels and Oreos, in the first place. I knew she only wanted me to be happy and that, in losing weight, I'd be happier. I knew that she, like me, only wanted to do what was asked of her, by anyone. So she stayed silent when I continued to order the chicken fingers platter at Pizzeria Uno rather than a salad. She bought desserts because I loved them, regardless of rightness. But still, I knew her desire for me to lose weight was there. And I wished it weren't. The outside world made me feel imperfect enough that I didn't want to feel judged inside my home, as well.

I continued to attend group meetings, and I began to hate them more. They were a tiresome commitment. An early-Saturday-morning reminder of how fat I was. In the remaining two months of the study, my weight stayed mostly the same. When it ended, I continued eating as I always had, only now, the taste of the foods I loved were laced with bitterness.

Through the rest of eighth grade, I gained another five pounds. But Mom? She lost thirty with a combination of walking on her lunch breaks, eating smaller portions, and her tiring work schedule. She'd ask me to go for a bike ride with her, and I'd say a firm no, because I was already running out of motivation; a ride around the neighborhood couldn't help that. She did what I had only dreamed to do. She did what she dreamed for me to do. She was radiant. More alive, more energetic. She was as light, as bright, in presence and mind, as she was in body. I envied her. I'd watch her wear the clothing from the Gap that I eyed on mannequins. I wanted so badly to tuck my shirt in with such ease. The way she carried herself reminded me of old photos I'd seen of her from the early 1970s, when she modeled. Her confidence became disarming. Her glow dulled me somehow.

The following winter brought my first formal dance as a freshman at Medfield High School. That ninth graders were even allowed to attend the same dance as upperclassmen was enough to ensure that everyone in my grade bought a ticket. Boys wore well-starched shirts, jackets, and ties; girls wore long gowns and high heels and got their hair done. The whole fall was abuzz with excitement as my best friends and I fantasized about December and dresses and dates. I was almost able to be thoroughly thrilled, except for one thing: it was a Sadie Hawkins dance. The girls asked the boys.

On one hand, I knew that if the boys had to ask the girls—as it was with traditional dances—certainly no boy was going to ask me. I'd learned early on, at Friday night middle school dances, that no matter how straight I blow-dried my hair, no matter how sparkly my Bonne Bell lip gloss, no matter how hard I made them laugh in English or math or social studies, no boy asked the fattest girl in our grade to dance to one song, let alone fifteen of them in a row.

But on the other hand, I knew that if I was the one doing the asking, I had a better chance of someone saying yes. It took me three weeks of November to decide whom to ask. And then it took six days of unrelenting anxiety to muster the courage to ask him. When I dialed his home phone number and he answered, I momentarily thought of hanging up and never going to school again. But no. The words came out of my mouth, "Will you go to the Christmas dance with me?" And in the second before he responded, I grabbed a handful of fat on my waist and squeezed it firmly, wanting the pain I inflicted on myself to hurt worse than what I was sure was a more painful rejection to come.

"I'd love to."

I about died. I thanked him, hung up, played my Mariah Carey CD twice through, and kissed my Leonardo DiCaprio poster no fewer than three times. It wasn't until the next day that the high of having a date settled down into a sort of bittersweet satisfaction. I hated—but couldn't help—thinking that even though he'd said yes, maybe he'd done it because he didn't want to hurt my feelings. I hated thinking that maybe he would still be embarrassed about going to the dance with the fattest girl.

Still, I was glad to be going. Kate, Nicole, and I went to the mall to look for dresses. After thirty minutes, four horrible dresses, and three turns standing in the large and unforgiving three-sided mirror, I was no longer interested in looking. None of the dresses—not even sizes sixteen and eighteen—zipped. None even came close. What was more embarrassing than having to acknowledge that I couldn't squeeze into the most matronly of women's dresses was that Kate and Nicole were simply stunning in everything they tried on. They pulled off the most shimmering of pastel gowns, the salmon-hued silk numbers I'd wear if I could. If only silk loved me even a smidge as reciprocally. They pulled aside the curtains to their dressing rooms, and I noticed wide smiles first. Their hair was thrown casually into messy and unforced romantic, low-slung buns, their shoulders shifted back in confidence, their arms hung like long, graceful frames for a lithe silhouette. The dresses—surely sewn with them in mind—fit gorgeously.

And there I stood, smooshed inside a two-piece, floor-length taffeta construction that fit my figure so poorly that I had to ask for help getting it onto and off of my body. I saw the flab bubbling over the strapless top where my boobs met my armpits and introduced them to my shoulders. I felt the waist cinching, an antagonizing corset reminding me of my belly. And then I turned to the side to view myself again in that terribly honest tri-fold standing mirror, sucking in my gut with breath held tight, as if a one-inch displacement of my mass was going to make a difference. I judged the dress I'd squirmed into, like all the rest, on a scale of one to five: one being "I'm wondering if that trash bag in my trunk would be a touch more flattering" and five being "This dress does not make me want to vomit and/or write hate mail to the designer." I winced. I wasn't unused to this. Years and years of trying on too-snug clothing with best friends had left me knowing that my shape was always more of a hindrance than anything else. Buying anything felt like choosing the lesser evil. *Nothing fits as I'd like it to, as magazines illustrate things should, so what can I live with? Which shirt will be more forgiving? More concealing?*

I left the mall that day with no dress and even less confidence. I decided to try again at losing weight. This time, though, I moved more. I experimented with that place where people went for self-flagellation: the gym. And at the end of a month of an off-and-on, loose-as-a-goose plan, I only weighed more. I went to the dance larger than I'd been in the fall. I had a dress tailor-made at a bridal shop—a purple dress that cost Mom three hundred dollars that we didn't have. Worse than the small fortune she paid, I didn't even remotely love it. The empire waist made me feel as if I were wearing the latest in formal maternity. The eggplant hue made me feel like the vegetable itself. When we posed for the professional photo, I stopped breathing as my date stood behind me and put his hands on my hips. I was mortified thinking he might feel the girdle I'd worn underneath my gown—the one that cut off the circulation between my abdomen and my thighs. And when we picked up the pictures at school the next week, I wanted to burn them in a ceremonial hate fire along with that dress and the awful rhinestone studs I'd asked the hair stylist to tuck into my updo. The eight-by-ten alone made my eyes prickle with tears. Sharing half of the photos with my date at his locker felt as if I were giving him photos of me in the nude.

After the dance, I spent a week gorging on every food I saw. I ate straight through Christmas and clean into the New Year. My self-esteem had fallen to a new and seemingly bottomless low. I realized the food wasn't making me feel any better, but even still, I stuck with the habits I'd created long ago.

I promised myself I'd try again to lose weight.

When winter break ended and ninth grade resumed, I tried out for the girls' lacrosse team. Thankfully, it was less of a tryout and more of a "we're going to accept anyone." After our first practice, where we were instructed to run suicides across the field, I went home and threw up from exhaustion. Running with what felt like a knapsack of fat left my knees in agony. Gasping for air left my throat hoarse and dry and my lungs racked with sharp, icy pain. On top of being terrible at the sport and winded from a light jog to get my water bottle, the uniform was a horror show. The shirt, even in extra-large, barely made it around my midsection, distorting and somewhat obscuring the letters as they stretched to either side. And the skirt. The skirt barely covered the place where my thighs mingled and chafed.

That whole spring season—despite falling in love with being part of a team—I dreaded all the practices, all the games. I knew that my body would not only fail me physically but also embarrass me. And the fatigue made me hungrier. Rather than wanting to eat healthy things, I found myself ravenous and unable to control the kinds and the amounts of food I was eating. Pizza, ice cream, cookies—they were rewards for hard work, for putting myself out there. I gave up on losing weight when I realized that the very thought of trying to cut back sent me into panic attacks, which sent me directly to the candy aisle of CVS.

By the time sophomore year came, I was diet weary. I'd already attempted downsizing a dozen times. I'd gone to a Weight Watchers meeting with Kate's mom, who also wanted to lose weight, and I'd cursed myself for half of the meeting, knowing that no one else in the room was under thirty with no children. I feared discovering that any of the women at the meeting was a mother of one of my classmates. I worried that she'd tell her child she saw me, with the other Medfield moms, at a diet center.

One week of tracking my meals and counting points in my head at the school lunch table, and I felt like a loser. I resolved to buy a salad every day, only to end up pouring ranch dressing on top as though it were water on a fire. I knew the points ascribed to creamy dressings, but I wasn't always competent at eyeballing a two-tablespoon serving or willing to stop there. I went to the YMCA after school to work out; it was the only gym in the area where I was certain no one I knew belonged. I weighed myself daily just to see if I'd made any progress, any progress at all, and no. Nope. None.

Again, I failed.

As people around me started dating—as my best friends started experiencing their first kisses and started going boy crazy—I felt more like an outsider than ever before. I wasn't teased any longer; I wasn't being bullied. But I was still painfully aware of my fatness and all the ways it excluded me from normalcy. I began to withdraw, often eschewing invitations to hang out and instead retreating to be on my own. I built walls around myself with bricks of cake, using frosting as mortar.

A really frustrating part was realizing that being boy crazy wasn't even a worthwhile pastime. You can't be boy crazy if no boy would ever be crazy for a girl like you. You can't fantasize about your first kiss if you can't even imagine that a boy—any boy— would kiss you.

And so instead of moving on to healthy adolescent relationships with boys, I clung to my childhood crush. While my friends were kissing boys, I was kissing that poster of Leo. I pined for someone who wouldn't have the chance to let me down, someone in such a castle-in-the-sky of a world that I knew he couldn't concern himself with real-world flaws.

At sixteen, I'd reached five feet nine inches tall and 210 pounds. I'd all but given up on myself, when Mom found out about another medically run weight loss program. I was reluctant. I detested dieting. But I detested my body more, and that alone was so potent, it compelled me to try again. This time, the plan was to consume a mostly liquid diet. Two high-protein shakes and one reasonably healthy meal per day. Though it sounded an awful lot like a more expensive dabbling in Slim-Fast, Mom trusted it was more legitimate. She always trusted these medical programs. They were created and facilitated by doctors, after all.

I lasted four days. I was too embarrassed to bring a shake to school for lunch because—who brought a shake to school for lunch? Preparing them required ice and a blender. Drinking them required forgetting the pleasure of all other food. I'd wake up frequently throughout the night, hungry from the lack of snacking after dinner. I'd feel light-headed and moody. Mostly, I missed chewing.

I had come to a place, three years into a cycle of dieting and bigger than I'd ever been, where I believed I'd qualify for gastric bypass surgery. Mom believed it, too. She assured me that if I thought it was something I needed to do, we'd find a way to pay for it. The potential financial guilt aside, I thought, long and hard about going under the knife, about downsizing my stomach and removing much of my intestines, as my only hope for health. It never felt right, though. Some part of me knew I had to do it on my own, or at least that I hadn't yet exhausted all my other, less extreme options.

I found myself with a muddier relationship to eating than ever before. Until I was thirteen, I ate with reckless abandon, using food for every reason unbound to hunger. But through my various concerted efforts to change the only body I'd ever known, I was accepting that all of what I'd been was less than ideal. I was trying to lose weight on the surface, but deeper, I was acknowledging that I'd been wrong for sixteen years and had to work to right myself. *How do you walk away from all you've ever been?*

I felt tethered to the food. Beyond having grown up believing that food and eating were expressions of love, food came to exist as the only thing in my life that was mine and mine alone. She comforted me; she filled in the hole where a dad might have been; she puttied the cracks of a broken heart; she stayed home with me when no one else would, when no one else could; she let me make decisions all by myself; she promised I was in control when we were together.

And better yet, she loved me. More of her meant more—of everything.

When I failed at all the many diets I attempted, I proved I couldn't keep promises I made to myself.

I realized, *I'm always going to be the fat girl.*

4

THE SILVER LINING of resigning myself to being fat was the sense of acceptance that came with it. I learned quickly that my submission didn't mean giving up; it simply meant moving on. I would still be fat, but that wasn't the only thing I had to be. And so, even as my weight remained stagnant during all of junior year, everything else around me thrived. My circle of friends expanded, I had my first boyfriend, and Mom fell in love.

At the beginning of the school year, I met with a guidance counselor to discuss my plans for college. I'd had my heart set on the University of San Diego for a while, and I fantasized about living in the sun and warmth of California. Years earlier, Anthony had visited San Diego while on break from school in Arizona. He returned, raving about how beautiful it was and how perfect the weather was all year long. "You'd love it," he told me, describing the beaches, hills, and canyons with such detail that I was able to picture them, like postcards. From then on, I dreamed of going and thought school would be my chance.

There in the counselor's office, I watched as he inspected my transcript. "Well, you have a solid GPA," he started, eyeing me through the glasses that rested on the bridge of his nose. "That's the good news. What you need now is more extracurricular activities."

After the meeting, I walked slowly down the hallway to my next class, mulling over his advice. I knew that he was right; I'd have to get more involved in order to have a better chance of getting into a school like USD, but the very thought of putting myself out there overwhelmed me. As the fat girl, it was much easier to pass through high school quietly and unassumingly. Joining clubs, playing sports, being active in highly visible social circles could make me vulnerable—potentially open to more judgment. But those things could also facilitate gaining new friends and new experiences. They could allow me to leave our lonely little apartment, and that reason alone was powerful.

I began by rejoining the lacrosse team—a comfortable starting place, since I'd played the year before. In time, as I gained more courage, I volunteered to manage the varsity swim team; joined peer mediation, peer leadership; worked nights at Casabella, a small pizzeria uptown; got elected to student government; and sat on the planning committee for prom.

Surprisingly, it felt good to throw myself into so many activities. I reconnected with Kate and Nicole through lacrosse and swim team, and as a tight group of three we met even more friends. I learned about what it felt like to be ambitious and outgoing and social. I laughed more. Through all of this, I started to gain some confidence.

When working in groups, I didn't hesitate to interact with anyone, even the popular kids. Guys like Mike Oppel—undoubtedly the most handsome of our eleventh grade, and perhaps the whole of Medfield High School—weren't as intimidating to me as they once had been. But Mike was a special case. Funny yet solidly good natured, he was the one who played dodgeball best in gym class; who made jokes often, but not at the expense of someone else; who charmed girls and teachers alike, just by smiling. The two of us had shared a few classes during middle and high school, and because 'O'ppel sits a few seats just behind 'M'itchell, so did we. We were friendly, but not "friends."

The emerging ease I felt—with friends, with school, with guys—was affirming. And none of it was connected to my weight. In some ways, deciding to just accept my fatness gave me a way out. A way to exist without bullying myself as others had. Because acceptance, tainted with sadness or not, is acceptance nonetheless.

And as I felt my life beginning to change, Mom's did, too.

One year earlier, Nicole's parents had divorced. That break, and all the painful changes that come with a split family, hurt Nicole and her two younger sisters deeply. Her mom, Peggy, and her dad, Paul, attempted to maintain some semblance of normalcy. The yearly camping trip that Paul had always invited me and Kate to tag along on was one tradition kept intact.

Paul and Peggy had known Mom as an acquaintance for years—since the year we moved to Medfield and Nicole and I had become friends. Now, with the camping trip approaching, Paul asked Mom if she'd be willing to come along to help with the five of us girls. After careful consideration, she said yes. Mom already spent any free time she had outside of work with Nicole, Kate, and me. We'd go to the movies or out to eat; we'd lie all together in her king-size bed and talk with her honestly about boys and friendship and life. We could go to her with anything, and she'd listen. Her closeness with each of us gave her a second-mother status among my friends, and Paul knew that.

A week out from our camping adventure, Paul invited Mom to dinner at his apartment to plan. Together, they ate from Chinese takeout boxes and made lists of supplies to pack. Until that dinner invitation, I hadn't seen Mom go anywhere that wasn't related to work or me or Anthony. I couldn't remember the last time, if ever, that she'd received a dinner invitation from anyone.

She came back from the meal talking as if she'd made a friend. For the rest of that week, they shot phone calls back and forth, tying up odds and ends in preparation. I knew there was a purpose to the calls, but I sensed there was something more going on when I heard a new tone to her laugh, when I saw a blushing smile after she'd hung up. By the time we set up camp in the woods of New Hampshire, it was as if the two of them had been good friends for years. They seemed a well-suited pair, laughing and commiserating as they wrangled the five of us kids.

Mom and Paul stayed in touch after we returned home. Every week, Paul invited her over for dinner to catch up. He always cooked—hearty comfort meals like beef stew and London broil steak with mashed potatoes. I grinned when she came home from his apartment the first time he made her his famous spaghetti and meatballs, glad to know that she had found them as unbearably delicious as I always had. She was so happy; for the first time, some-one was making dinner for *her*.

I adored Paul. And I loved that Mom had found someone to spend time with; I really did. But I struggled with it, too. It was downright foreign for her attention to be divvied up between me and anything other than work. As she got ready to go out with him, my mood turned pouty and irritable, and I was unable to let her go without forcing at least a twinge of guilt. I wanted her to feel remorseful for leaving, but then the second I noticed in her eyes the inner battle she fought before heading out the door, I was ashamed. While it took some getting used to, the longer they dated, the more comfortable I became. Observing how much they'd grown to love each other softened me. I noticed the ways in which the two of them were alike. Like Mom, Paul had a massive heart—one that made him so unreservedly generous, loving, and kind that you'd take him for a big pushover if you didn't know that he also had a rule-loving, stern side, too. But where Mom was often extreme, disorganized, and chaotic, Paul was mild mannered, calm, and collected. Where Mom was emotional, he was rational. They balanced each other.

After a year together, they bought a house in Medfield, and Mom, Paul, and I moved under the same roof with an almost seamless transition. Nicole lived there part-time, and Katie and Caroline, his two youngest daughters, came over for dinner once a week and slept over two weekends per month. By then, I loved him. I loved him for the pure and decent man that he was, for the good, kind soul within him. I would have been content to just adore him as Mom's partner, but, blessedly he chose to love me back. He packed lunches for me to take to school in the morning; he made sure we had dinner as a family at night; he drove me to and from the doctor, the dentist, the orthodontist; he treated me the same as his own daughters. He provided stability in a home that for so long had lacked it. Not a day went by that I didn't marvel at my luck to have him around. Not a one when I didn't have to wonder who this man was who treated me with such profound kindness. I didn't take him for granted as I'd often done with Mom. Paul was a gift.

But not everyone felt that way. Anthony struggled with Mom's new relationship. He butted heads with Paul, feeling threatened that another man had stepped into such an important role in his family. At twenty-four, Anthony was too old to be fathered by him, and too hurt from our own dad to trust another one. They fought constantly. The same things that I was grateful Paul could offer us—stability, structure, and security—Anthony resented and rebelled against. Oftentimes, Paul's rigid sense of order and rightness washed over Anthony as judgment. I could see that Anthony never felt he could be fully himself, at least not without a worry that he might be perceived as weak or inferior or lazy. Whenever he'd live at home—which was usually for brief periods of time in between jobs and apartments after moving home from Arizona—shouting matches would ensue. The painful part for me wasn't seeing Mom torn between the two of them; it was seeing Anthony's eyes when he believed she was choosing Paul over her son. It was that he sometimes looked at me as if I were a traitor, and that he hated me for the way I'd taken to loving Mom's boyfriend. It was the sadness that I had found a father figure and he hadn't.

And Anthony wasn't the only one who struggled. Nicole, too, had trouble seeing Mom and Paul together. She pulled away from me, distressed by seeing her dad moving on and not knowing how to reconcile that her relationship with Mom—the woman she'd come to love as a second mother—was changing, too. She resented me when it felt as though her dad were becoming mine.

She wasn't ready for all the changes, and my heart ached, knowing that one piece of my life was coming together while another was falling apart. The only reason our relationship survived high school and into college was because we both tried desperately to ignore the changes going on around us and continue as the friends we'd always been. We pretended that everything was all right—even when it wasn't.

In late March, Nicole's mom went away for the weekend, leaving an empty house. Nicole, Kate, and I did what any seventeen-year-olds would do: we threw a massive party. We invited thirty friends over, locked up the valuables, and bought jumbo packs of red Solo cups. That we were in a house rather than the woods of Noon Hill was already a step above the usual Medfield nightlife. There was confidence in my voice as I reassured us, "We'll just clean up so well tomorrow morning that no one will ever find out."

Now, having seen all those high school rom-coms, one would think that at least one of us would have anticipated the debacle when fifty people showed up to the party, nearly doubling the original count. None of us foresaw the beer caps that got flicked far out into the yard off the back deck, to be discovered later by a gardening parent. None of us expected the mess created by sloshing booze-filled Solo cups across the kitchen linoleum during rounds of flip cup and beer pong. Instead we forged on, temporarily muting that annoyingly accurate sensibility alarm, and one hell of a party was had by all.

We awoke the next morning bleary-eyed and disheveled. We cleaned, we scrubbed, we scoured the yard for cans and caps and Mike's Hard Lemonade bottles. We disinfected and deodorized as best we could. In an hour, the three of us had turned the place from Animal House into an HGTV model home. And when we were done, we decided a greasy breakfast at Bickford's diner at one thirty in the afternoon was just what we needed. In Nicole's bedroom, we changed out of our party apparel and into whatever we saw first in her dresser, not having brought our own change of clothing. For Kate and Nicole, choices were cute graphic tees, hooded sweatshirts, and yoga-type stretch pants. I, with blurred vision and a keen internal radar system that helps me detect the biggest sizes among heaps of clothing, picked up a badly beaten mauve thrift shop sweatshirt with a crew neck and a few worn holes that was loose and clearly four sizes too big for Nicole. To match, I pulled on charcoal sweatpants—the kind with tapered ankles that your nana might own in seafoam, lavender, and beige. I would have loved to have made a joke about them if they hadn't been so tight, but they fit almost in the same snug way that the yoga pants fit Kate. My look was a curious mix of bohemian meets mistake. Chubby and boxy, I'd have been better off in something a little more fitted than that sweatshirt. Big has a funny way of only growing bigger when it mixes with baggy.

After brunching on Belgian waffles with home fries and maple sausage links at the diner, the three of us headed to the high school lacrosse game to say hello to friends. By the time we arrived at the field, the game was half over. Our friend Alexandra, a striking, leggy blonde, stood across the field, waving for us to join her. I squinted to make out the faces of the rest of the circle, realizing Mike Oppel was among them. Walking over, I felt that familiar fat girl dread. In my head spun, *Of all days to forgo makeup, this had to be the one, huh? Suck it in.*

I hated the feeling of walking toward people, and of walking away from them even more. I was aware of my rolls, the way the elastic waistband of Nicole's pants cut into my fifth layer of love handle. I thought of Mike's eyes—everyone's eyes—watching, running up and down my body, seeing the flabby parts of me that I would kill to photoshop in real life. The indigo undereye circles that Dad had genetically gifted to me. The extreme roundness of my face, only made more moonish by the fact that I'd not yet deeply side-parted and straightened my hair that day.

I was unprepared. I couldn't have been further from the ideal I'd like to present to anyone, much less Mike Oppel. The field seemed threatening now—to me and my quite unhelpful mauve sweatshirt.

As we approached, the group turned to welcome us. Of the six that stood before us, I was casually friends with each. Alexandra let out a sweet "Hey!" and we returned a chorus of weary "Heeeyyys." Chatting about the night before and the now half-over game, I began to feel less uneasy. By that point, I'd reconciled with the fact that there was no more that I could do to make myself look better in that moment than smile and be kind. We'd only be there for a few minutes anyway.

Nearly back to the car, I felt the pat of a hand on my shoulder. I swung around to see Mike; he'd jogged to catch up to us, trying to get my attention. I let go of a small giddy squeal and smiled wide before panicking at the realization of what an overeager weirdo I'd just been. I was altogether too exhilarated to be stopped by him, considering he probably just had some question about class.

"Andrea!" he said. "Hey! How's it going?" He stuffed his hands into his pockets.

"It's going pretty good. A little slow moving today." *What is this?* "How about you?"

"Good. Things are good." He looked down, searching the ground as if to find another topic of conversation, and when he spotted one, he looked up again. "So, I was wondering—are you going to the prom?"

"Um . . . well . . . yeah. I mean, I don't know . . . but I'd like to," I said hopefully.

"But you're not going with anyone yet?"

"No."

"Cool." He nodded and paused, thinking on it. *Well, this is an all-time low,* I thought. I wished I could have sprinted off the field, done anything to escape the awkwardness of not only admitting to Mike Oppel that I was dateless but also showing him how gross I could look on random Saturday afternoons.

"Will you be my date?"

I flatlined.

I jolted back to life just in the nick of time to answer his question with the most mortifying three words: "Are you kidding?"

The confusion on his face introduced me to my own absurdity. "No . . . ha. Why would I be kidding about that? I want to go to the prom with you."

I scanned his expression, picking it apart for a hint of an impending smile that would expose the ruse. My head whipped around to look across the field, certain this wasn't actually happening. I felt a curious mix of vulnerable and high. As the tiny hairs on my arms stood up with a tingle, I lost the ability to control the deep smile that made its way from my belly to my heart to my head. Completely disarmed, I looked down at my sneakers, wiggling my toes before raising my eyes to meet his once more. "Uhh. Y—yeah. Of course. I'd love to." My face flushed rosy.

"Great. Awesome." He smiled.

I bashfully tucked my hair behind my right ear and made one last pitiful error in playing it cool. "Thank you," I said, sincerely. He laughed while shaking his head. "No, thank *you*. It'll be fun."

I pivoted on my left leg, swiveling around to face the parking lot, where my friends sat in Nicole's car, anxiously waiting. I walked to them in a dreamy, bouncy stride. My whole body felt warm and fizzy like a shaken bottle of soda. My smile continued, unrelenting and uncontained. What had just happened was outrageous, a little too high-school-coming-of-age-film to feel true.

For the month leading up to that sunny May prom day, I went about my life in pure, almost transparent delight. I moved through the halls of Medfield High with a new level of confidence.

Yes, there were moments of panic, times when I second-guessed and self-sabotaged and stalled my own happiness. Mike Oppel's asking me to be his prom date brought all sorts of insecurity to the surface. *Is he sure about this? Do you think he regrets it? Have his friends teased him or made jokes about the date he chose?* It was easy to pick apart.

But I chose to feel lucky. I lingered on my high. I felt lustful just imagining the possibility of more joy than I was already experiencing. A month before the big day, Mom and I headed out to a bridal shop that sold plus sizes forty-five minutes away from home in a small town on Boston's North Shore. After finding not one forgiving fit at Macy's, Filene's Basement, JCPenney, or David's Bridal, this was our last hope.

We walked into a tiny store jam-packed with gowns in every

shimmery shade standing tightly in single-file lines along every wall. Rows and rows of taffeta and tulle snaked around us, ranging from hot-tamale-red silk to jade-green satin, and all manner of sparkle and sequin.

The owner emerged through a draped door at the back of the shop. Warm and smiling, standing a petite five feet tall, she looked me up and down, nodded, and said without hesitation, "We find something, my dear." Her thick Italian accent, her reassurance—they rubbed the back of the hopeless girl in me. I smiled.

She and Mom sent me to the dressing room—which was more of a sewing room, with barely a suggestion of a door—with three dresses in tow. I eyed each and stopped immediately, gasping at the blue silk one. Floor length and strapless, the dress flowed smoothly, gradually changing from a sapphire hue to indigo to topaz to where the hem flared into an icy blue A-line. I set aside the other two dresses, not even noticing color or cut, and took my clothes off. The weight of the dress Hula-Hooped around my head, swirled down my neck and back, and then settled at my waist. It was two sizes too big—a twenty-two when I'd normally worn an eighteen. Still, I loved it. I knew it would be perfect.

Before I could even spin to see all sides of me in the mirror, the shop owner had flung open that whisper-thin door, took one look at me, and tossed her hands up in the air. "Thee one," she cooed, tilting her head to the side in contentment.

I pivoted back to the mirror, beaming. I took in the image of me in that blue. "Yes. The one."

Mom wrote a check for the dress without even blinking. At $250 before significant alterations, it meant three weeks of overtime and sleep deprivation just so her baby could be the belle of the ball. When I hesitated at the register, swallowing the price like a handful of rocks, she took my face in her hands. "You can't put a price on feeling beautiful." I looked into her eyes, so loved and in love with her, and smiled through tears. She pressed her plum lips to my right temple and whispered, "You are worth every penny I have, baby. Every last one."

The drive to prom with Mike felt seconds long. Our chatting, laughing, sparring back and forth with playful jabs was effortless, comfortable. I was myself and he, himself, regardless of social status. And what I won't ever be able to forget is the feeling of strolling into the prom venue, arms linked with Mike Oppel, *the* Mike Oppel, and for the first time experiencing exactly what I'd wanted.

To be seen.

To be seen as beautiful.

It was a strange feeling. Foreign. The heads—polka dots of slick crew cuts and hairsprayed updos—turned as we walked past. Friends ran up to say giddy hellos, each leaning into my ear to whisper "You are gorgeous!"

Our entrance and pure kindness from everyone we encountered as the evening began sent me spinning. We ate dinner, danced, and then, just as the lights dimmed, our principal took to the microphone at center stage to announce who had been voted prom queen. Our class nominated only a queen, and whoever her date was became her king. All of us gathered on the dance floor, whispering in anticipation. I looked around, pausing to admire all the girls in my junior class—each absolutely radiant in some shade of spring. I wondered which would be crowned queen, grinning as I eeny-meeny-miny-mo'ed my way through them. Turning to Mike,

I leaned into his ear. "Who do you think it'll be?" He leaned back, looking me in the eye, his pupils scanning mine back and forth as if to answer silently. He let out a sweet laugh. I narrowed my eyes, searching his for more information. *Did he know already? Could he know?* I felt jealous if he did. I returned my gaze to our principal, my mind trying to select someone immediately so that I'd at least be a betting woman before the announcement, even if only with myself.

"I'm thrilled to announce that this year's junior prom queen is . . ." Our principal pulled a thick card from the envelope. Eric Clapton strummed the first few chords of "Wonderful Tonight," and I heard it.

"Andrea Mitchell."

Ahem . . . Excuse me?

I looked around at the others, clapping and cheering, looking straight back at me. *I'm sorry, I didn't catch that. Who?*

Clapton crooned, his voice dragging, sultry, across sweet lyrics. *"I say my darlin' . . ."*

As the principal crowned me, my face stained beet red. Mike took my hand and pulled me toward him. He rested his hands at my waist, and I brought my arms to his shoulders, intertwining my fingers at the nape of his neck. My cheek brushed his. "You look beautiful," he whispered into my ear. I felt my blood coursing through all the veins that led to my heart as it swelled. Pressed together, we swayed to the music. I squinted from the spotlight directed at us and saw the hundreds of faces that encircled us—each adorned with a smile. It was a scene cut from a movie.

And I—for the four minutes of that song, that sweet slow dance—was not just the fat girl.

I was beautiful. I was prom queen. I was accepted. I was weightless.

The song softly faded into the next, and the clapping resumed once more. My friends rushed over to hug me. People I'd never spoken to came up to congratulate me. The outpouring of kindness was dizzying.

My high lasted for five hours of dancing and laughing. Five hours of feeling as if I were floating. Five hours of pure, boundless euphoria. Five hours until my rational mind brought me back to reality.

At our all-night after-prom party, many people stuck close to their dates, but Mike and I floated around the crowd separately. I saw him from across the room talking to another girl—a strikingly beautiful girl. I noticed the way he smiled as he talked to her, as he flirted with her. And I realized that none of those smiles were ones he used with me. I saw that none of his actions—the way he stood, the way he brushed arms with her—was anything like how he was with me. I did my best to shrug off the realization and moved into the adjoining room to chat with friends. Over the next few hours, I had so much fun playing drinking games that I'd all but forgotten about Mike and the girl. He had come over to me a few times to see how I was doing, and, with an arm wrapped around my shoulders, he'd asked if I was enjoying the party. I'd light up at his touch, at his sweet concern. I couldn't help but adore him. "Yes, I'm having the best time!" I'd enthusiastically reassure him. He'd smile, relieved at my contentment, and then he'd leave me. Each time he walked away, my heart grew heavier. Knowing that there was another girl in the next room pained me. I'd look down into my beer cup, watching embarrassment float to the top, as unwanted as foam. *Did I think he liked me? Did I really allow myself to think that Mike Oppel had any romantic feelings for the fattest girl in our grade? How had I deluded myself into thinking he invited me to prom for any reason other than wanting to be generous, kind, even?*

I left the room and found my way to the bathroom. There, in quiet solitude, I felt silly. I was a good deed done by Mike Oppel. An ironic prom queen. I wondered if my win was meant to read as *Let's do something nice as a grade and vote for this big girl. Let's give her this one.* I felt as if my whole class had secretly nominated me for a makeover and cheered as I came onstage transformed and oddly confident. Charity, for which I should have been grateful.

And I was. The boost in self-esteem, the elation—they were crowned upon me. Even if they came with their own sad interpretations, I was just glad to have them at all. The choice to view the night in a positive or negative light was up to me.

When I was finally able to leave the bathroom, it was because I couldn't bear the thought of reducing my happiness to tears. I walked outside to refill my drink. Seated on the grass surrounding the beer cooler was a big group of people. I found an open spot and sat down beside my friend JJ, our class president and also the guy I'd had a crush on since the fifth grade. He turned his body to face me. "Hey!" His massive grin could make me forget that I'd been upset mere minutes earlier.

"Hi!" I returned, equally as enthusiastic.

"Congrats on prom queen. That's really great."

"Thanks! Yeah. It's—it's strange. I don't know how that happened." I laughed.

"I do. I counted the votes, and it was pretty much unanimous. Everyone wanted you to win." Hearing him say that made me feel good. I smiled.

For the remainder of the night and well into the morning, the two of us sat in those grassy seats and talked. Our only pauses were the minute-long laughs we shared, reminiscing about all the years we'd gone to school together. It was intimate, the kind of lengthy and meaningful conversation I'd had with Kate. I didn't fear saying the wrong things; I didn't waste precious mental energy worrying whether he was silently wishing he was talking to someone else; I didn't spend time wondering how disheveled I looked in the morning light. Candid and a little irreverent, I was myself.

By eight a.m., it was clear we should head out. I placed my palms flat on the ground at either side of me, preparing to stand up.

"You know, I've thought about telling you—," he started. I stayed seated, looking him in the eye. "I had wanted to ask you to prom." He looked serious, vulnerable, and my pulse quickened.

Blushing, I cast my eyes downward. "Oh." I paused, shifting nervously in the grass. "Well . . . thank you. That's really nice."

He released a small laugh. "No, nothing to thank me for. It's just—you're great, and it would have been fun."

A rush of exhilaration surged through me. "The good news is that we kind of spent the whole party together." We both laughed.

"You're right." He nodded. "And it *was* fun. We should do it again sometime."

I grinned, revealing how happy what he'd said had made me.

The next day, he called to invite me to the movies. The day after, we spent the better part of an evening driving around aimlessly in his car, talking in the same way we had a few nights earlier. Our friendship grew fast, my liking of him building quickly and intensely.

After a month of hanging out daily, we had a conversation that revealed how deeply we liked each other. And on our second "official date," I had my first kiss. It was everything I'd imagined it could be. Fireworks and an encore of Dave Matthews Band. An overabundance of perfume and braces. He was wonderful. Sensitive and kind, outgoing and funny enough to make everyone enjoy his company. For six blissful months, including an amazing summer, I was happy. As continuously content as I'd ever been. He wrote me love letters and poems. He made me mixed CDs—the second-surest sure sign of love. He never once made mention of my appearance, save for calling me beautiful.

And the best part? I had someone. Finally, someone. I was validated. I was worthy of love. All 210 pounds of me.

One week before my birthday, in January of my senior year, the two of us went out for a drive. It was just a normal outing until tears began to fall down his face. He turned to me, and I anticipated exactly none of what he said. I was horrified thinking that perhaps someone he loved had died, that he didn't get into his number one choice of schools. Instead, he broke up with me.

And my love, everything I had handed over to him in moments of intimacy, felt lost. He cried as I did, there in his car, assuring me that he still loved me and that he always had. It was just that he didn't want to be in a relationship. Stripped of security, I couldn't hear a word. I knew it was me he didn't want. It was all a kinder, gentler way for him to say he wanted out.

My heart was broken. I spent three weeks tearing apart our relationship, hoping that there had been a misstep that could be corrected, like fixing a measurement in a faulty recipe. All the conclusions I came to pointed directly at me. I was fat. Maybe it was my size that had outgrown our relationship. Maybe he was getting teased for dating the fat girl. Maybe he'd begun to find me gross.

The more time I spent dwelling on these theories, the more solidified they became. And when graduation came, several months later, I thought of myself as being as unattractive as I'd come to believe he'd found me when we'd broken up in January. I'd gained 10 pounds in those months, bringing me to 220.

Not until late that summer, ten days before we'd each be leaving for colleges on opposite sides of the country, did he and I meet up one last time. Driving together, late one night, I felt the comfort of our old relationship. We talked, familiar and smooth like vanilla ice cream. Just as the sun began to rise, he told me what he hadn't been able to tell me in January. He told me what he hadn't told anyone. He told me what he barely wanted to say aloud to himself. He was gay.

I'd never before felt the way I did in that moment. Shock swirled with relief mixed with a quarter cup of heartache. There was a knowledge that it would never work between us, that it simply couldn't work between us, and with that came sadness. There was an acknowledgment that it wasn't me who he found unlovable, and with that came relief. And suddenly it all made sense. Why we never quite made it past second base.

And after a moment of recognizing all these mixed emotions, I reached for him. I wrapped my chubby arms around his lean swimmer's body and tried to make him know that I loved him in that embrace. What I felt wasn't any longer about me. It was compassion—pure and tender—and admiration. I couldn't help but respect the bravery that he had mustered to tell me. To tell anyone. I couldn't help but feel a deeper connection after such honesty, such vulnerability. And for that, I loved him more. Deeply, but in a different, oddly fuller way.

In the fall, I would begin college at the University of Massachusetts at Amherst. I hadn't been accepted to University of San Diego after all. When the rejection letter came in the mail, I was crushed. Out of the four schools I applied to, USD was the only one I'd really pined for. It was also the only one outside of New England. Only slowly, as friends decided on schools in Connecticut, Vermont, and Rhode Island, did I begin to come around to the idea of staying close to home. I rationalized that going to UMass, my safety school, would be much cheaper than the others I'd considered, and in the end the lower cost swayed me. When Nicole picked UMass, too, I felt even better about my choice, and the two of us decided to room together.

I had spent much of the summer hoping to lose at least a few pounds, but with the endless graduation parties, farewell dinners, and daylong shopping trips for college necessities, I always found an excuse to eat everything. The night before leaving for college, I packed up the last of my shirts and, eyeing the XL on each, stuffed them into a duffel bag.

Someday, I promised.

5

I HAD JUST MOVED THE LAST SUITCASE into my dorm room on the sixth floor and said a sniveling good-bye to Mom and Paul when I met him. My orientation schedule had made it so that I moved in a day earlier than Nicole, and I missed her when I saw the swarm of freshmen and their parents in the hall. Everyone sported the same anxious and overeager smile that I wore. The campus of University of Massachusetts is massive—so massive that I hesitated at the thought of having to head to the dining commons by myself for dinner, unsure I'd find my way back to my dorm without a map. On the one hand, I wanted to be the outgoing person I'd grown to be and introduce myself to make new friends. But on the other, I wanted to avoid the awkwardness I felt when I could see others surveying me for the first time, when my weight greeted them before my handshake.

I ran into him outside my door, walking the length of Grayson Hall and wearing a fitted Red Sox cap. When we made eye contact, I panicked momentarily, not knowing whether to stop and say hello or not. *This is how you meet people* was all I could think. "Hey! I'm Andrea. It's nice to meet you." He sent back a laugh at my formality, turning his head to the left to dodge a box being carried past him. I eyed him up and down. Five feet eleven inches and strawberry blond, he stood solidly at my door. He was chubby, too, and for that, I felt safer.

By the end of the first week, Nicole and I had made fast friends with two girls on our hall. There was Jenny, the sweet and hilarious one from Cape Cod, who also happened to be the object of affection for seemingly every guy in the dorm. Then there was Sabrina, a small and busty brunette from Jersey with striking dark features, pursed lips, and razor-sharp wit. I took a liking to them instantly. It began with us simply walking to and from the dining commons, where we'd tell hilarious stories about the odd characters we'd met in our dorm and then retreat to one of our rooms to watch old episodes of *Dawson's Creek*. But in no time at all we were inseparable. We'd rearrange our schedules just to walk one another to classes; we'd take naps together in cramped twin beds; we'd talk constantly throughout the day; we'd get ready together to go out on Friday and Saturday nights; we'd laugh hard and often. There was nothing casual about it; we were obsessed with one another. And I was grateful for them.

Living just two doors apart, Daniel, the guy I'd met on my first day, and I passed each other dozens of times a day. Nicole and I had become friendly enough with him that he'd stop by our room to say hello, hang out, or grab something to eat. I couldn't get over how funny he was. No one could. His humor made people comfortable, and it made him popular. Everyone knew his name. He'd make the sharpest, pithiest observations I'd ever heard, and laughter would pour out of me, heavy and uncontainable, as full and thick as an upended gallon of milk. I'd laugh so hard, tears would fall down my face, so hard I couldn't breathe. That kind of elation made me want to be around him more often. Oddly, it seemed the only thing that made Daniel laugh was me. He poked fun at my mannerisms, my eccentricities, and even though I rolled my eyes, I secretly liked seeing him smile. I liked hearing the gentleness of his laugh compared with mine. I noticed that the bits of me he deemed quirky were some of the same ones I found weird to the point of annoying in Mom. And somehow, that made me feel strange and comforted all at once.

Two Fridays into the semester, a big group of our new friends had congregated in the student lounge for a party, and I realized that Daniel was not only funny but brilliant, too. In the middle of some conversation about our majors, the guy who'd been endlessly spewing jokes and witticisms since I'd met him revealed he had more brains than he let on. He told me about his choice of major—journalism—and waxed poetic about writing, language, and literature. The way he referenced *The Elements of Style*—one of only two books he'd toted with him to college, alongside Salinger's *The Catcher in the Rye*—impressed me. *What guy packs these kinds of things?* I wondered. We compared class schedules to find they were almost identical in our choices of anthropology and film history. We drank in conversation rapidly, as easily and eagerly as we did the Pabst Blue Ribbon.

Hours later, just as the moon got woozy and let the sun tuck her to bed behind the hills of Amherst, Daniel and I said good night. Alone in my room, in that extra-long twin bed with a candy-apple-red comforter, I smiled, thinking of the new friend I'd made. Getting to know Daniel was like taking one bite into something

I couldn't quite place. It was layered and complex, an unfamiliar taste I liked enough to crave more of instantly. Perhaps what lured me most was that it was never enough to feel sated. There was always a gentle nuance to him, something new I'd just begun to discover.

Months passed, and we grew closer. We walked to and from our film classes, lunched together at Franklin Dining Commons—his plate composed of a cream cheese–schmeared pumpernickel bagel beside a bowl of minestrone soup and mine a children's menu mainstay: chicken fingers with french fries. And come Thursday evening, affectionately known as "Thirsty Thursday," we partied together—as loud and long as the start of a weekend would allow.

Out of all four girls in our circle, without his needing to confirm it, I knew he liked me best. It was our chemistry that kept me confident, the way we'd sit for half a night in the elevator lobby, long after all had gone to bed, and talk about everything from Martin Scorsese films to our mothers, to the worst meals at the dining commons.

It wasn't until Valentine's Day, one month into our second semester, that I sensed a shift in our connection. My girlfriends and I, each of us single and sappily sad to say so, lay in a pile of hugging bodies on my and Nicole's pushed-together twin beds cooing over the movie 13 Going on 30, cry-singing "Love Is a Battlefield," and eating pink-frosted Dunkin' Donuts. Daniel dropped in to find us tangled together, alarmed at what a broken mess a group of girls could become when so taken by a Hallmark holiday.

"I've got just a little something for you. It's nothing much, but considering how crazy you guys are about this silly day, I think you'll appreciate it." He handed Jenny, Nicole, and Sabrina tri-folded sheets of printed paper. Turning to hand me mine, he smiled and left the room with a nod and a gentlemanly bow.

As soon as the heavy door clicked closed, we unfolded them feverishly. We sat in silence for a few minutes as we read the personalized messages. Each of us had our own love poem, a favorite of his by poets he admired. The stanzas sat squarely at the top of the page, leaving the bottom open for a paragraph or two of his own writing. Sabrina's, Nicole's, Jenny's—they were sweetly worded and heartfelt messages that let them know how special he found each of them, how unforgettable his time had been while knowing them. But mine. Mine had only one sentence tucked below the poem "elaborate signings," by Kenneth Carroll.

elaborate signings
(for Joy)

"women are the sweetness of life."
poets can build galaxies from pebbles
& breathe the word of life into brief glances,
but one must be careful with the power of creation
so i scribble an obligatory, struggling to keep from
staining the page with the exaggeration of new passion,
unsure if i am simply the writer who lives downstairs,
plays his coltrane too loud & likes thunderstorms

i take a trip one flight up
where your eyes escort me to another country,
your touch becomes a wet kiss on the horizon
of a birthday in a warm july
i travel to your smile to hear stories of
wrecked trains parked in your dining room

but the past is a vulgar thief
it steals the laughter from your eyes,
tosses the broken edges of yesterday's heartache
into this remembrance
i dream of erasing painful memories with lingering
caresses from a steady hand

i rearrange the jagged stars of your past
i am the young boy smiling at you with love letter eyes
i carve your name into the soul of graying trees
i am your first slow dance, a trembling hand teetering on your waist
i replace the melancholy prayers on your lips with urgent kisses
i swear an oath to your beauty, become holy in your embrace

traveling tall miles through years of distance,
i arrive, wet from your tears,
my only tool—a poet's skill
i mend your smile,
emancipate your eyes,
& together
we ride that wrecked train from your dining room
to the horizon of your birthday in another country.

And below, in four words, he had penned,

"You are beyond words,
         —DJW"

I reread the poem. My heart, my whole body, tingled, a jump into a cold pool after steeping for hours in a hot tub. My eyes darted back and forth between the lines, replaying my favorite parts. In a state of shock, I tried to look back in my memory for signs that had led to this. I remembered the times we sat in the elevator lobby after dark, me telling him about my dad and a liquor-laden girlhood and he admitting that his own mother was a heroin addict, now only a fragment of what she once had been. We commiserated, both of us exposing hearts that had torn, ripped, and lost pieces. I let him in. He knows what I know. We were kindred spirits.

I noticed I had been holding my breath. I exhaled, blowing out the air in a controlled stream to steady myself.

If ever I've had a moment where I felt downright cradled, just absolutely embraced by someone's actions, it was then. Reading and rereading that poem—a gift from a man who knew me well and had decided, nonetheless, that I was wildly worthwhile—I felt loved.

His added note at the bottom, though only four words wide, was lines longer in meaning. There was an odd satisfaction, a certain pride in knowing that, although kind to each of us girls, he was rendered a touch speechless when expressing the way he felt about me.

It felt doubly validating for someone to have chosen me as his favorite among a slew of what were undoubtedly desirable girls.

Later that night I saw him. A group of us sat circled in my dorm room amid a landfill of red plastic cups and grease-soaked D.P. Dough calzone boxes, while Jay-Z threatened to call my RA for yet another noise violation. Unsure of how to react to his love letter, it took a whole thirty minutes for me to find the courage to glance his way. He leaned back in my desk chair, balancing precariously on its two hind legs, laughing as he played the perfect devil's advocate in a hilarious argument with Justin, his best friend as well as ours.

He should consider practicing law, I thought. Dad had been the only other person I'd ever known to be able to defend or defeat a point as masterfully, as convincingly. I remembered the way Dad challenged anyone, everyone, to spar with him in wits. How he'd never just let me win at anything—from miniature golf to Monopoly—for the mere sake of winning. I should earn it, work for it. And I craved that sweet, albeit annoying, know-it-all twinge of nostalgia Daniel gave me. Midstare, his gaze met mine. A half smile was all we could spare. But still, we acknowledged a moment. I sensed an unspoken agreement between us that we meant more to each other than the company we kept.

Weeks passed in a seemingly ordinary fashion. We talked as we always did; we bickered and bantered back and forth. And then, one Friday night, as we stood in the stairwell of Grayson, I handed him my feelings, certain and sudden as a baton passed in a relay.

"I'm in love with you," I revealed.

When he hesitated, I swished the cup of Captain and Coke in my hand. He pressed his lips together, looked down, pivoted to stare at the left entrance to the stairwell, and let out what I knew to be a remorseful sigh. "I . . . I, wow, I just—it's just . . . Andrea, I don't feel the same."

On his last word, I looked down and found my heart had deflated and fallen to the tiled floor.

"Oh" was all I could muster.

"I'm sorry. It's—I mean, I really care about you. I just don't love you . . . romantically."

I felt my chest tighten, my defenses rising. I left the stairwell before the conversation, the explanation, could constrict any more around me. Before it could leave me any more exposed and vulnerable. I heard the door close, and I knew he'd stayed behind, giving me at least a five-Mississippi head start back to my room.

How? I mean, well, I can't . . . how could I have misjudged it so?

How could I have put it all out there like that, so confidently? Bubbling tears slipped out from the corners of my eyes.

Of course, I thought, looking down at the belly that caught those tears. *It's this that keeps me stuck. It's this that leaves me unlovable.*

But then I thought of his body, his chubbiness, and I felt angry. Here I'd thought we were on the same level, both of us big, but maybe all this time he'd thought himself to be better than me because he wasn't *as* big. I no longer felt reassured by our mutual fatness. The rejection stung.

I spent a week thinking I'd really ruined things between us. All the days that followed, I avoided our usual spots. I went to a dining commons that was farther away; I would leave immediately after class without pausing to talk to him; I stayed busy away from our dorm. *Maybe he'll pretend it's all okay,* I soothed myself. *Maybe he'll think I'd just had too much to drink.*

When we met again that Saturday night, in the eight-by-ten-foot box of Justin's dorm room, hands cupped around beer cans, we said "Hey!" as casually as could be among friends. *Don't make it weird, Andie.*

We moved swiftly through small talk, confidently into our comfortable jokes. The tension seemed to break apart, scatter into pieces on the floor. Daniel and I had successfully swept our previous conversation—the one in which I pronounced love and he sighed—under the rug. *Onward,* I thought.

Our friendship returned to a state of normalcy. Classes, lunches, deep elevator-lobby chats, and laughing, always laughing. I almost forgot that night and the heartbreak. I was inching closer to "over it" territory, assuring and then reassuring myself that we'd gotten past the discomfort, the awkwardness.

And then summer came. And with it, forced time apart—with

Daniel back in Worcester and me at home in Medfield. We kept in touch online, chatting via instant messaging all night. And then one Friday night, when a party in the woods of Medfield ended earlier than we were ready for, Nicole and I decided to drive west for a visit with Daniel. In her mom-ish silver wagon, the stereo blaring Dave Matthews at peak volume, and with all windows open, we drove the forty-five minutes to his house. It wasn't until we were two streets away that I noticed the butterflies. The anticipation of seeing him somehow made me dizzy. We knocked quietly on his front door, sure that his dad would be asleep at two thirty a.m.

"Hey!!" Nicole whisper-yelled.

We each hugged, reuniting for the first time in three weeks. Arms wrapped around me solidly, he stayed in our embrace a little longer than I'd anticipated. It felt as soothing as seeing my mother coming to pick me up from a friend's house after a sleepover spent homesick.

We spent the next few hours in the living room watching Dave Chappelle's stand-up special on Comedy Central. He and I sat beside each other on the worn blue sofa while Nicole reclined in its matching La-Z-Boy. I looked over at her when I could no longer hear her laughing at the barrage of jokes. She was leaning to the side of the chair, face smooshed into its rolled arm, fast asleep. My eyes shifted from Nicole to Daniel, whose eyes were set squarely on the screen. I turned back to watch. Seconds later, just as my laugh started rolling to a boil at Chappelle's "purple drank" bit, I felt Daniel's hand cup over mine. I shivered, not having expected such a move. I turned to face him and saw he was smiling, too, head thrown back forcefully for a full-body laugh. When his eyes met mine, we paused. *I adore you,* I thought to myself.

It was then that he leaned sideways toward me. Face inches from mine, his breath warmed the air between our mouths. My whole body tingled. I felt the hint of his lips hang hesitantly, lustfully, nearing mine.

"I missed you," he whispered.

I moved the remaining eighth of an inch and pressed my lips to his. With that, a lit match tossed herself recklessly into a stream of propane. An instant heat. Neither of us pulled away.

"Did I fall asleep?" Nicole asked groggily, startling us and breaking our lip-lock.

She wiggled herself upright in the La-Z-Boy.

"Well, shall we?" she said. "Bet it's, like, four o'clock now."

"Sure. Yeah, let's head out." I looked to Daniel, and his eyes smiled into mine. My heart beat in my throat. *I love you,* I thought.

His stare replied with what he didn't say aloud. *I love you, too. And, really, I have all along.*

All through the next year, our sophomore, we dove in deep. A week before summer break, I sat in my dorm room uploading pictures I'd taken on my camera the Friday before. Each photo was funnier than the last. I smiled looking at each one. My whole college experience until that point had met almost all my hopes going in. The intense and meaningful friendships I'd made, the freedom and independence I gained while living away from home, the complete immersion in an environment that fostered and encouraged learning—all of it had exceeded any expectation I'd ever held about college and growing up. I'd even fallen in love, which I hadn't dared hope for.

But one very, very fat piece of me remained unhappy. I could see it in the pictures, even if my grinning face said otherwise. I'd gone up two pants sizes, and I could see the extra rolls that had baked on my sides, the way my belly hung over the waistband of my jeans like the downturn of a frown. I hated to see how much bigger I'd gotten, how inflated my whole body had become. I cringed when I saw the balloon that had become my face. In every photo, I was twice—and sometimes thrice—the size of all my friends. The clothing that I spilled out of was shameful to me. Nicole, Jenny, Sabrina—they looked sexy in tank tops and flouncy, low-cut blouses. Their shirts showed cleavage on purpose, whereas mine tore open trying desperately to contain me.

I never wore the black silk tank top I had on in that photo again. Not after the last time—the night the photo was taken, when the girls and I had gone to a party at SigEp, our favorite frat house and the only one to serve unlimited "jungle juice." The whole evening had the makings of a great memory: we ordered a takeout "party-size" pizza from Bruno's; we spent an hour getting ready together in Sabrina's room while blasting a killer playlist and sipping mojitos; we laughed and danced until exhausted and sweat soaked on the dance floor of SigEp. But then, about ten minutes after leaving the frat and trying tipsily to make our way home, it all turned sour. We'd decided to take a different route back to the dorm and, in doing so, passed by a row of off-campus houses hosting rowdy parties of their own. Inside the house just ahead on our right, people could be seen in every window, and rap music thundered out of the front door. A group of guys stood out front. Feeling friendly, Nicole called out, "Heeeey!" as we slowed our stride. The guys turned around, and the tallest one stepped forward, immediately returning Nicole's enthusiasm.

"What are you girls up to?"

We stopped there on the sidewalk while Nicole explained in her friendly way that we'd just left SigEp and that we were on our way back to the dorms. It was a gift of hers to create a conversation with anyone, and it seemed her charm had found us a new party to rock. That is, until one of the guys on the lawn shouted to us.

"Hey you!" His eyes were on me. I smiled and started to toss a hello back his way.

"No fatties allowed!!"

It was a swift kick to my stomach.

Paralyzed, I remained locked there on the sidewalk, unable to act on the urgent desire to run. I looked at the group of guys, three of the four bent over laughing hysterically. In an instant, Nicole unleashed a string of expletives, slaying the guy who'd hurt me. I feared she'd punch him when I saw her inching closer. Jenny and Sabrina hooked arms with me, pulling me forward to keep walking toward our dorm. I latched on to Nicole, so grateful to have her armor in that moment when I had none of my own. I dragged her away with the rest of us. "I'll be all right" was all I could manage.

I let my hair fall in my face to hide my tears. Nicole wrapped an arm around me, pulling me into her body so that my head nearly rested on her shoulder as we walked. She tucked the loose strands of my hair behind my ears. I loved my friends for the way they tried to change the subject, for the chatter they maintained during the whole agonizing walk home—a valiant effort to distract me.

Looking at the pictures of that night, the humiliation came rushing back. And with it, an almost suffocating truth: the bigger I grew, the smaller I felt.

In classes, no matter how strong my opinions, no matter how

innovative my ideas, I now couldn't bring myself to raise my hand, fearing the attention it could draw. I stayed silent and unassuming in the back of the classroom, in a desk that hardly fit me. On Tuesdays and Thursdays, if I found myself running late to the lecture hall, even by just five minutes, I was compelled to skip the class altogether, knowing that few things were as anxiety-inducing as trying to squeeze through tight rows of fellow students to find the lone open seat.

I thought that my relationship with Daniel, my first experience of true and pure romantic love, would fulfill me in a new kind of way. I thought that it would solve something, would satisfy some inner craving I'd had for love, and I'd finally start to lose weight. Instead, in growing closer to him, I got fatter. And at first I wondered if it was the security of having found love that kept me fat and made me feel comfortable enough to grow fatter. I questioned if it was the satisfaction of acceptance or the fact that my partner enjoyed overeating as much as I did. We had a similar relationship with food, after all. Every dinner out involved everything from appetizers through desserts. We'd split a large buffalo chicken pizza and an order of onion rings before heading into the darkness of the movie theater, my purse packed with enough chocolate to stock a convenience store. And though we had never discussed it, he seemed to share my desire to eat so extremely.

With Sabrina, too, I ate.

On one of the last nights of the semester, before summer break, she and I were driving around Amherst in her Jeep. It was our late-night routine—talking, singing with the windows down, drinking iced coffees with milk and sugar. And now we were in the process of collecting a very ordinary midnight meal. We'd already swung through the Dunkin' Donuts drive-through, where I'd ordered a sausage, egg, and cheese on an everything bagel and a vanilla cream-filled doughnut along with my coffee. Sabrina had ordered the same bagel sandwich without the egg. Our next stop was McDonald's, where I heard Sabrina yell into the little speaker box for "two large fries, please!" as I sat in the passenger seat and debated a McFlurry.

We drove away, a bevy of paper bags in my lap, and we ate, still singing at the top of our lungs in between bites of fry and bagel. And somehow, in the middle of our conversation or our song or our laughter, all the food was eaten. I looked down to see my last fry, picked it up, brought it to my mouth, and chewed it slower than I had the rest. When I swallowed, I turned to Sabrina. "You know, I don't think I like McDonald's fries at all," I said. She laughed. I laughed. It was an interesting realization, considering the fact that I had ordered those fries upwards of seven hundred thousand times in my life. I ate them regardless. When the next song started to play—a slower melody than the ones before—we got quiet, and I thought about what I'd just told her. About the fry revelation. I wondered how many other foods I ate that I didn't even like. Then I wondered, however briefly, if my eating was even about liking the food at all.

What I really enjoyed was the time with Sabrina—bonding over our favorite music, having long and sometimes profound conversations, and growing to know and love her more deeply. Eating recklessly was simply one more thing that brought us together. I liked the ease of eating with her and the fact that she ate similarly, though admittedly less. We looked alike, too, with jet-black hair and olive skin, even though she stood nearly a foot below me. But four feet eleven suited her. And while she was slightly overweight, she was fully Italian in her voluptuous butt and big chest. I only looked fat. I had no pronounced butt, no hips, no perky chest, just evenly distributed mass.

In our group of friends, none of us was thin—except for Jenny, and we were able to quarantine her as an anomaly. Jen ate what I imagined a high school guy eats while playing football and running track six days a week. Then she'd take a nap. And yet she was able to wear midriff-baring shirts that exposed a taut, flat stomach.

Nicole, the second thinnest, was a modest fifteen pounds over-weight, which by my standards seemed ideal. She ate as much as she wanted—cheesy breakfast sandwiches and bagels with an inch-thick schmear of cream cheese—and still looked great.

My three closest girlfriends and I, though we varied in thick-ness, appeared to eat roughly the same. Our routines aligned in similar patterns. Sleep, eat, class, eat, class, sleep, eat, bathe and beautify, party, eat, sleep. Repeat.

With them all, it was never strange, never embarrassing, when I called Bruno's takeout line twice weekly for a ten-inch pizza and a large side of onion rings, or when I tipped the delivery man for a two-person box of boneless fried chicken wings with extra blue cheese. Or even when I ate brown sugar and cinnamon Pop-Tarts on the ten-minute walk to the dining commons where we would get breakfast. All of us seemed to eat so massively, so excessively. If I was eating, they were, too—though perhaps not the same foods, in the same quantities. I can hardly remember an instance of feeling bashful when suggesting that we drop by KFC for a light snack of biscuits with butter and honey. In all of my life, the friends I'd kept had always been eaters just like me. We were second-serving-grabbing, lick-your-plate-clean, can-I-get-an-extra-scoop-of-that eaters. We wore our affection for food as a badge of honor, as though eating wildly indicated fearlessness. As though eating big meant living big.

And though I would have sworn I was on par, I undoubtedly had to have been eating more than anyone for the pounds to pack on me as they did. I look back now and wonder what sort of denial must have obscured my vision.

When the four of us went shopping at Holyoke Mall after classes let out on Fridays to find cute outfits for the coming weekend, envy was all that fit me. I browsed the racks at Forever 21, tugging at each stretchy top I came across—independent of whether I liked the cut or the style—to see how much the fabric would give, if it would drape over my rolls well once I managed to shimmy it down past my shoulders. It was just like in high school—only my options were really narrowing at this point. In the end, I was relegated to the plus-size section of Old Navy, which was not only more expensive, but frumpier, as well. Nothing that I ever left the mall with was what I'd have chosen if my size hadn't been a factor.

A few weeks before I left Amherst for the year, Mom drove from Medfield to take me out to lunch. I hadn't seen her in three months. She pulled up to the front of my dorm and waited there, at the curb, for me to come out and meet her. I pushed open the double doors and saw her tan Camry, instantly feeling the comfort of that squeaky-braked familiarity. Her face was just as I'd remembered it, un-made-up except for a thick lacquer of plum lipstick. A potent mix of Shower to Shower body powder and Clinique Happy wafted out from her open window to greet me.

As I reached down to tug on my stretchy camisole, the one that loved nothing but to ride up my sides, our eyes met. I smiled widely before realizing she wasn't smiling back. Something unfamiliar clouded her eyes, something uncomfortably different than what I'd expected to find in our first reunion. Her lips parted, and her jaw dropped slowly, like a cherry sliding from the summit of a melting ice cream scoop. Just before the cherry dropped completely, she snatched it up, her mouth closing into a thin smile.

Her gaze was fixed on my belly. I swallowed hard, almost unable to get down the growing knot of self-consciousness. Last time I saw Mom, I wore a size eighteen, and now, a twenty-two. As I moved closer to the car, she smiled purposefully to let me know how happy she was to see me. I smiled, too, but faltered when I noticed her eyes scanning me up and down, pausing as they reached the widest part of my abdomen, just above the tight perimeter of my jeans. I knew as she stared there that she saw what I did when I'd looked at those photos. My body was like a mushroom, with a stem of legs much too small to hold such an overbearing cap. The more I thought about it, the tighter I contracted every muscle, every fiber in my belly. I sucked air and held it, as if being a fraction of an inch slimmer could vindicate me.

I was stunned by the foreignness of what I saw in Mom's eyes. She, for the very first time, revealed the shock, the panic she felt about my size. It was the first time she hadn't been alongside me as I grew, so the change was more blatant. And maybe for much of my life, she'd accepted that I'd always been fat going on fatter, but now—wearing a size I bought secretly so no one would know—I was the fattest. And it scared her.

Until that day, that moment when I felt like a stranger in her eyes, she had been my sole source of comfort. She was the one who loved me unconditionally, who saw me as beautiful regardless. In the past when she noticed my weight, her worry seemed entirely empathetic, a way of loving me in my struggle. Now, it seemed grave.

She never said a word about it. Not at lunch, not on the phone later that evening. But I knew. She knew. Seeing her so shocked, so full of despair at how fat I'd gotten, knocked the wind out of me.

6

I LEFT SCHOOL THAT MAY praying that this time would be different. That this would be the summer my weight would finally pack its bags and leave for good. That I'd never again see that look in Mom's eyes. I desperately wanted to feel ready for change, to be empowered and resolved and committed, but mostly I was terribly scared.

By the time I'd arrived home late on Friday afternoon, I'd already planned to start trying to lose weight on Monday. And just as I'd done in the past, I launched a massive "farewell to fat" binge. That weekend, as I unpacked in my bedroom for the summer, I ate all I loved, taking care to fit in all my favorite foods before I'd start trying to lose weight on Monday. Entire rows of Double Stuf Oreos, twin packs of Little Debbie Swiss Cake Rolls, a Roche Bros. chocolate cake, a ten-inch Meat Lover's pizza. I ordered a half-dozen Dunkin' Donuts—two French crullers, a Boston cream, a Bavarian cream, a chocolate glazed, and a coconut—pretending casually and coolly to the cashier that I was bringing the box home to a hungry family of four. I cracked open can upon can of Sprite. I rang the Taco Bell.

On Monday I walked into the women's locker room of the YMCA with Kate. I was relieved she'd decided to join me. She took our bags to an open locker while I headed to the corner that housed the scale. Dread settled over me as I stepped on it.

I never thought the needle would stop winding around that center dial. My eyes had taken to the polish—fuchsia and fiercely proud of it—neatly laquered on my toes. *I should repaint those. Some shade of coral, though, this time.*

Standing on the metal platform, so white and sterile, I braced myself. I had no hopeful number in mind, no fingers crossed. And even as a bigger than big girl for two decades, I felt unprepared when the needle slowed near three hundred pounds. *Really? No, I mean, let's just be clear about this. Really?*

I stepped off the scale, waited a beat, then repositioned myself back on, just to be sure of the number.

Two hundred sixty-eight.

The metal under my feet dampened. My heart picked up tempo. I breathed in too shallowly to steady me.

Two hundred plus sixty plus eight.

I don't like that number, I thought.

It wasn't the two hundred that scared me so; I had seen those numbers before. It was that I sided with three hundred now.

How did . . . How could I . . . When?

Hang on a sec . . .

What?

I held my breath and wondered if closing my eyes might help to slow a now-spinning room.

I had known big. In fact, I had only known big. But this

number—those three earned digits—was sobering. Seeing it there, black bold on the starkest of white, tangible and true, I wanted to cry.

Standing there on the scale, I couldn't ignore it all. Each pound was real and, worse, inescapable.

I thought back to the look on Mom's face when she visited me at school. I remembered the terror in her eyes as she saw my declining health. Now, being confronted with the reality of the scale, I shared her concern. I saw myself with the same scared eyes.

The whole of me was terrified, a complete and uncondensed definition of overwhelmed.

I stepped back, lowered myself from that brutally honest scale, and looked to Kate, who stood behind me. I could tell that she hadn't seen the number, but she'd gauged from my expression that it was bad. Her eyes expressed compassion. There was nothing to say. I managed a halfhearted smile, and in an earnest attempt at perky, I asked her, "Well? Shall we?"

We walked from the locker room to the main floor of the gym. Treadmills, elliptical machines, and stationary bikes lined the far wall. Free weights and Nautilus equipment formed an obstacle course before us. Each of the machines I passed appeared more foreign than the last. Bodies bared before me, none resembled mine. Even the most out-of-shape gym attendees strode confidently on an Arc Trainer, seeming to me a reasonable forty pounds from fit.

I was out of place.

I scanned the cardio options, eyeing each in a way to ask, *Which of you will make me feel least hopeless?* Or better yet, *Which of you promises not to tell everyone here that I have no idea what I'm doing?*

The elliptical seemed best. For thirty minutes, I moved; my

arms pushed and pulled in sync with the gliding of my legs. And even though I'd set my machine on very little resistance, I felt beat by the time it kicked into a two-minute cooldown. *Thank you,* I thought. Sweat dripped, hot yet quickly cool, down the line of my spine. I felt the wet beads that were collecting on my scalp steam my naturally curly hair into a frizz of spirals. Blood rushed to flush my cheeks and tingled down my legs, unused to such rigor.

There was a moment where, in between relieved gasps of air, I felt trapped on that machine. *Is this what it's like to get, to be, to stay, thin?* I wondered. I was sure I never wanted to relive those thirty sweaty minutes. I glanced around me at the others. Sweat suited them. Their faces, so focused and willful, expressed they were as tired as I felt, and yet their determination was intact. Grunting as she finished her final seconds of sprinting, the woman on the nearest treadmill smiled in a relieved, proud way. *What's different about her and me? How does she finish, looking strong and confident, while I, the one who needs to be here as badly as bad can be, finish thirty minutes feeling exhausted of spirit?*

I stepped off the elliptical. I looked to Kate, who was as over the whole workout as I surely was. I felt thankful she shared my discomfort. We walked back to the locker room, the two of us feeling released from prison sentences.

"Well, that was terrible," Kate confided.

"Yes," I commiserated. "Yes, yes, and a hundred more yeses. Is this how our summer will be?"

"No, it won't be this bad. We'll get used to it."

I nodded, wanting dearly to believe her. I would have given anything to have been in Kate's shoes. I would have given anything to have wanted to be at the gym for the plain and simple reason of getting in shape, as I'd seen Kate write on the fitness questionnaire we were asked to fill out when we joined. *What must the people working the front desk have thought when the two of us walked in together?* I wondered. *The blond one's here to tone up; the brunette's here to overhaul her life.* I had to stop myself from dwelling on it too long, for fear that resentment might brew.

Ten minutes later, I slouched beside Kate in her Mercury, the air conditioner blasting, our bodies already aching.

The sweat glossing my face began to dry in a tight, tacky way. I pushed the radio dial and found Britney Spears's familiar purr. We listened, not needing to say anything beyond the exchange of a few reassuring smiles. She knew I was tired. I knew she was tired.

I looked out the window and thought of that scale. The number. The needle nosing almost as far as the machine would allow. For the first time, in all of my bigger-than-big life, I felt afraid.

I ran around my brain looking for a space just big enough to fit the blame. *Damn that food.* All that I'd eaten in twenty years came to mind, as lustfully, as vividly as pornography. Thick, rose-middled burgers, gooey with melted cheese and between sesame-seeded buns. Dripping butter pecan ice cream cones. The grease spots remaining after all the slices of a pizza pie had up and left their cardboard home. Potatoes—french and twice fried. Fingertips smudged a fiery Cheetos orange. The glossy yellow trickling onto my movie theater popcorn. Raspberry jelly oozing from the side of a powdery puffed doughnut. The corner of a sheet cake.

I struggled between wishing away all the food that had collected on my body as fat and fiercely missing every morsel. I hated the binge last weekend, and I wished I could do it again. I wanted to eat less, and I wanted immediately to eat more. I wanted to be angry but felt too hurt, too ashamed to thrash about. I wanted to fit in while also wanting, so badly, to say a careless "f- off" to all of society. I wanted to run each ounce off but felt more like taking up permanent residence under the covers of my bed. I wanted to be alone while wanting desperately to be held tightly.

I knew I was large. I knew that the scale wouldn't ever have sided with svelte, but I hadn't braced myself for 268. Nothing could have prepared me for such a fact.

And what was worse, what was even more paralyzing than realizing that I was pushing 300 pounds, was that I couldn't close my eyes and make it go away. It wouldn't just disappear. Only exercising and eating right could help.

I compared myself to the spectacle of people I'd seen on television shows. The half-ton man; the woman who never left her house again; the panel of obese teens on talk shows; the mother who was forklifted from her home, from the bedroom and bed she'd taken to as refuge for years when her legs could no longer stand her weight. Every big person I'd ever seen, in the flesh or in film and photograph, flashed before me. *Is that what I've become? Or at the very least, am I on my way?*

I was the girl who needed an intervention, the one in denial of her size. I felt I'd woken up to a body covered in excess. Why didn't I stop sooner?

My motivation for losing weight had always largely been vanity. The health warnings I'd read in magazines, the ones I'd gotten from my pediatrician, seemed like idle threats to an invincible teenager. But as I approached 300 pounds at twenty years old, I was reminded of my mortality. I was no longer just big. I was obese, and worse, *morbidly so*, according to the height and weight charts

I'd read online. I had reached a point where I no longer distanced myself clearly from the others, those on television: the *really* big people. It was just as my doctor had predicted in eighth grade. And it wasn't just the peak I'd hit that stung. It was the numbers I imagined just past the peak. What lies beyond 268? Where do you go when you've only ever traveled northward on the scale? Though never particularly adept at math, I knew even on a very elementary level, that a safe prediction of my future weight meant 300 pounds . . . 315 . . . 330 . . . 345, and on and on.

The thick, solid black line I always imagined as separating me from the biggest of big narrowed and faded considerably. *You're not far from them now, Andie. A few years, and you'll be there, too.*

I stared at my belly. Two very unwanted bulges rolled down my front. My thighs, in the loose-fitting shorts I'd worn, were rippled with waves of cellulite. The seat belt dug diagonally between my sagging, chubby breasts. I cursed each ounce of flesh. As if the fat had arrived of its own accord and set up a commune on my hips, thighs, and love handles, I wished it would leave, quietly but quickly. In those minutes, losing weight felt all at once easy and impossible. I knew how to do it. Even a person with the most basic health knowledge knows that to lose weight: You must move more. You must eat better. And you cannot binge-eat.

When you've never been thin, never met normal numbers on the scale, you don't know that living in moderation is possible. My notions of thinness at that point revealed a stunted, misguided impression of all those who had bodies I admired. Half of the thin folk, I assumed, survived on salad. They ate sparingly and almost immaculately clean. This I imagined to be equally confining and elating, because being thin, after all, would be more satisfying than any food. The models, the hot Hollywood crowd—they all brought to mind immediately that common diet saying, "Nothing tastes as good as thin feels." I assumed it to be true. I already felt trapped, looking at a future of flavorless eating.

The other half of the thin folk I assumed were naturally slender. Raised by parents who did not struggle to eat moderately, they lived in bodies that regulated hunger and fullness with distinct signals, while mine had gone wonky. These individuals were more enviable, because whereas the former half of thin folk at least seemed to work to be bodily beautiful, this effortless half seemed to have won the genetic lottery. My genes were not so lucky. Dad, Nana, the people I most closely resembled—they waltzed straight past thick and stood squarely in fat. Those family members were future versions of me.

The thought shook me awake. A freezing cold shower seconds after leaving the warmth of bed. And yet I already dreaded the next day and the next exercise session. I made a mental list of all the reasons I couldn't, I just wouldn't, be able to keep it up. The excuses poured out of me. In minutes, I had ten fairly reasonable ways to defeat my own weight loss. I was lining obstacles up like traffic cones.

Kate dropped me at my house and leaned over to hug me.

"I know what you're thinking," I said. "And, yes, I almost always smell this good."

I opened the car door and stepped out. Bending down into the passenger window: "I can drive tomorrow. Pick you up same time, same prison."

She laughed. And with that, she reversed out of my driveway, and I made my way to the back door.

Sitting in bed with my laptop later that evening, I searched for body mass index (BMI) calculators and height-and-weight charts. Most of the information I found suggested that a healthy weight range for a twenty-year-old female standing five feet nine inches tall was, on average, between 130 and 170 pounds. To meet the high end of the range, I'd have to lose 100 pounds. I set my sights on weighing 140, but then part of me hesitated in pinpointing a number at all. I had no idea what my body would look like at any of the lower, healthier weights, and it seemed arbitrary to be so specific so far away. But I needed a goal to strive toward, so 140 it was.

The next day came and, with it, the gym. Kate and I pulled into our spot, the one inconveniently facing McDonald's. I stared in lust.

"I should just keep driving straight ahead. Keep going 'til we've broken through the golden arches and the deep fryer is in the front seat with me and the McFlurry machine is in the back."

Kate lifted her eyebrows and smirked, knowing the idea wasn't the worst I'd ever had. The scent of french fries wafted through our open windows, hot and salty as the summer air.

Sitting still in the driver's seat for a moment longer, I thought back to the most touching of all weight loss stories I'd ever come across. Two years before that summer, I was in the waiting room of my doctor's office thumbing through *O, The Oprah Magazine* (Oprah, if you're reading—because I know you like to read—I adore you always and forever). Midway through the thick issue, I found a piece written by a woman who'd lost one-hundred-plus pounds. She credited much of her transformation to the support of Overeaters Anonymous. For the first time, I had felt connected to someone who shared her struggle with weight and the grieving associated with trying to eat less, to limit yourself. The writer was honest; she was vulnerable line after line in a way I hadn't heard before. The part that stood out to me, as if highlighted in neon yellow, was when she recounted a night she felt particularly weak in her resolve to not binge-eat. She called her sponsor in desperation, feeling herself slipping off the ledge of her willpower. Her sponsor paused, considered her pain, her anxiety and lust to binge, and said:

"Can you do it today? Can you make it through today without bingeing? Just today, and tomorrow we'll reconsider?"

The writer was struck, as was I in reading it over. "Uh, yes. I mean, yeah—yes, I can get through today," she stumbled out in concession. In that moment, she realized that this phrase would be her mantra. It would be the question she'd ask herself, day in and day out, when she felt herself falling back into old habits. *Can you do it today?* The notion of just trying to take each day as it came. The commitment to the present moment, and only the present moment, without worrying about the big and daunting picture of all the days that followed. The mustering of strength and dedication for now, if not later.

That question stayed with me after having read her article. And at that moment, sitting in my car outside the YMCA at the beginning of my own weight loss journey, it floated into my head like a banner attached to a blimp in the sky.

Can you exercise today, Andie? Not tomorrow, not the next day, not even a month from now. Today? Eat the best you can, work your plus-sized heart out . . . today?

And, I found, I could.

The first three days—when I sobered to the fact that my life would be devoid of a deep fryer and two-for-one doughnuts, at least for a while, anyhow—were almost unbearable. During the day, I'd feel fine eating healthily. I bought health-focused magazines at the grocery store and pulled sample diet menus from them to try on my own each week. I mixed and matched as best I could to find the kinds of meals I liked most. I didn't know the calories, the carbs, or the fat grams, only that the foods and portions in the meal plans were deemed healthy by whatever registered dietitian helped design them for the magazine. On an average day, breakfast was scrambled egg whites with a handful of baby spinach thrown in to wilt, one piece of whole wheat toast, and a cup of berries. Lunch was a salad with grilled chicken, feta cheese, and half a large pita pocket from the Greek restaurant up the street. Dinner was simply seasoned and grilled chicken, pork, or beef, served alongside a pile of steamed vegetables. Snacks were fresh fruit and anything labeled light, sugar-free, or fat-free. I had heard enough times about the myriad benefits of fresh fruits and vegetables to know that I needed to incorporate as many as I could.

Eating right in the daytime went well, but when the sun went down each night, I felt that deep longing for sweets. Come eight or nine p.m., my stomach felt hollow. I wanted cake. I wanted chocolate. I couldn't watch television without looking to my lap, where I wished there could be a bowl of crunchy something, anything. I couldn't deem the day done without having that urgent stuffed fullness. I needed to be sufficiently sugared for sleep. Anxiety, sweaty palms, my body writhing in discomfort. An addict, I cried, heartily and whole bodily, every night.

One week in, it got easier. And by easier, I mean I agonized less. Perhaps my stomach shrank, or my mind's appetite did, whichever comes first.

Daniel was forty miles away at his dad's house in Worcester for the summer. He had also gained a significant amount of weight during sophomore year, reaching nearly three hundred pounds. When he saw the steps I'd taken toward losing, he made the same commitment. Twice a week, we'd see each other and go out for healthy dinners, take long walks, and go to the movies, where our only shared snack would be a diet soda. I found tremendous comfort in having someone to go through the process with me. But, for him, it always seemed easier. His love of sports made exercise less of a chore. Daily, he'd find friends to play pickup games of soccer, basketball, or tennis. Combined with eating less, he lost forty pounds in three months.

I spent the rest of that summer following my own decidedly healthy path of exercising every day—taking group fitness classes, using the cardio equipment, jogging or walking with Kate—and trying to eat well. I lost just over thirty pounds in those three months of summer. I won't say it was fun, but I will say that, like anything new, and like any challenge you embark on, it was exciting at first to see the numbers on the scale fall. I had my best friend with me. And Britney Spears was still making music that moved me.

At the end of the summer of 2005, I went back to school feeling better about my body. Mom took me shopping for new outfits. Proud of my weight loss and mindful that she couldn't reward me with food, she showed her love with gifts. At the large outlet mall near our home, she bought me a new wardrobe to show off my smaller figure. Reuniting with old friends back on campus, I'd hear, "You look great!" or "Have you lost weight?" It was rewarding.

And though I continued my efforts to make healthier food choices, aim for smaller portions, and walk to classes a few times a week, I dropped my rigorous workout routine so I could focus on classes and socializing. Without my own kitchen, I wasn't preparing my meals any longer. Fruits and vegetables were scarce. Instead, I was lured by the familiar temptation of greasy late-night pizza slices, snacking to stay awake; Sunday-morning brunch plates pooled with maple syrup; and a constant influx of takeout in my dorm. Staying strong and committed seemed impossible when my environment was booby-trapped with indulgence. And to top it off, that fall, Amherst opened up a burger joint called Fatzo's that sold cheese-smothered Tater Tots and one particularly juicy "Cowboy Burger" that involved smoky hickory barbecue sauce, onion rings, and Monterey Jack cheese. I couldn't help but love it.

And then there was the matter of alcohol.

Even in the years long before Dad died, I swore I'd never take a sip of the stuff. Not a drop would cross my lips. I remembered all the ways it hurt Mom, scarred Anthony, poisoned Dad. I couldn't so much as look at a bottle of liquor without seeing it as a symbol of heartache. But as I got older, my drive to teetotal softened. In the years following his death, I learned more from Mom about how broken Dad was—that there was more than just the love of the drink at work. He had been abused as a child and suffered from crippling, lifelong depression. Alcohol wasn't the cause of his problems; it was his misguided solution.

I saw other adults in my life drink alcohol in moderation with no ill effects. At holiday parties, my uncles drank beer. Mom even sipped the occasional hard lemonade. Gradually, I stopped viewing alcohol as an evil to be avoided at all costs, and by the time I was sixteen, I, like most high schoolers, was curious to try it.

The first time I drank, Nicole and I had been invited to a house party after a Friday-night football game. Everyone would be there, I was assured. The invitation alone flattered me.

I enjoyed the feeling of a slight buzz, the mild euphoria, the way my inhibitions were cut free by Smirnoff. I liked the way laughter grew as the night went on, the way social status ceased to matter, the fact that after three beers all of us appeared thin. And mostly, while I had fun with alcohol, I felt no serious attachment to it. The part of my brain that lived in a steady state of worry and paranoia kept an eye on my boozy behavior. It reminded me of my past when it seemed I had forgotten. The one thing that left me sad, left me as guilty as I'd ever felt, was the thought of how much my actions might hurt Mom if she found out. I pictured her face, the grooves of lines made from years of worry, and I felt a secret shame.

When I entered college, I embraced drinking as an integral part of campus life. Booze bound us all socially. Nicole, Sabrina, Jenny, and I drank cocktails on Thursdays, on Fridays, on Saturdays. There was no getting around the party scene of college life. And more, there was no way I wanted to withdraw from it. The years I'd spent in Amherst were the most fun I'd ever had, and drinking, though admittedly illegal and five shades of risky, was as much a part of that as skipping classes to sleep in. I don't regret one shot or one hangover.

One year into my stay at UMass, I fessed up to Mom. I promised her I'd be careful, that I'd be aware of all the ways I could easily fall into genetically addictive patterns. And though she might have been choking back tears at the time, she knows as well as I do that I've always kept that promise.

* * *

When I returned to school at a lighter weight, I discovered other challenges I hadn't previously thought of.

On a practical level, I always lamented that being bigger meant more alcohol was required to get me tipsy. I lamented the calories. In the beginning of college, I'd drink six beers, even eight beers in a night. But once I knew that the alcohol, as excessive as it was in our social lives, would reverse any weight I'd lost if I didn't at least attempt to lighten what I sipped, I started experimenting. The girls and I took to mixing powdered sugar-free, calorie-free Crystal Light lemonade into a Nalgene bottle's worth of three parts cold water to one part vodka. We called it disco lemonade. I'm not sure if it was the cutesy name or the fact that we'd invented our own "healthy" cocktail that made us love it so; it certainly wasn't the taste.

Shortly after junior year started, my weight loss stalled. Or at least it seemed as though it had. My jeans weren't any looser; I wasn't noticing even the subtlest of changes in the bathroom mirror. I worried that I'd let two and a half months at school pass me by when I could have been working toward losing more weight. It was clear that I still had quite a long road ahead of me. I decided that I needed help to go on, so I joined Weight Watchers on the first day of November. Sabrina joined, too, wanting to lose a modest twenty pounds. Setting foot on the generic conference room carpeting of the meeting room, I thought back to the meeting I'd gone to with Kate's mom in high school. While it hadn't been a livable plan for me as a teenager, I wanted it to work this time.

Sabrina and I weighed in before making our way to the back to sit with the group. I steadied myself on the scale, anticipating failure. I feared I'd gained. And how could I not have, when I'd struggled so consistently to make the right choice in the face of temptation and nine times out of ten failed? When the woman recording my weight revealed it to me, I was shocked. I had lost ten pounds. I smiled at her, exhaling a sigh of relief, and I noticed the momentary look of confusion that flickered across her face. It took me a second before I understood her reaction. There were probably very few people that she weighed in who seemed happy to know that they weighed 228 pounds. But for me, 228 was progress. A 10-pound loss in two and a half months would have been nothing during the summer, when I'd maintained a rigorous workout regimen, but I knew full well how challenging the food and drinking scene at school had been. The fact that I'd lost 10 pounds sent a gentle ripple of pride through me. Simply the fact that I hadn't gained was a small miracle.

This time around, I took instantly to the Weight Watchers plan. After the first meeting, my motivation and commitment had been restored. Meticulous by nature, I loved the structure, the planning, the goals. It felt comfortable. Counting points taught me the fundamentals of nutrition and portion size—essentials I'd never known: that I should inspect ingredient lists for calories, fat, protein, and fiber; that quantity matters, and quality, too. I liked being given a framework—a quota of points for the day based upon my weight and height and goal—it was up to me to spend them how I wanted. Because, though whole foods are wonderful and lovable and all manner of virtuous, sometimes I wanted to use my points on a brownie rather than anything more nutritiously sound. Many times, in fact. I liked that a cookie could fit into my plan. No food was off-limits. Yes, cake costs more in points, but I learned to respect it more in turn. I learned to enjoy the moment when I'd chosen to spend five precious points on a lemon square, because they were special, earned, and loved in their spending.

For the few months that I followed Weight Watchers, I followed the plan on my own. Sabrina continued on her own, as well, and when either of us felt like giving up, we'd find comfort and strength in the other. Apart from two group meetings, I just felt more comfortable flying solo with my Point Tracker. Having always struggled with consistency in dieting, I began journaling what and how much I ate. This single act changed the way I viewed and valued eating, teaching me accountability and an awareness of my own hunger and fullness. I noted which times of day I felt most in need of sweets, which times were easiest and hardest. There was a pleasurable quality in reporting to the journal, to *myself,* what I'd put into my body. A Tetris-like game was born. I found ways to fit healthy foods and treats perfectly side by side in the same day. Each night, I went to bed with a deep sense of satisfaction for the confidence that came with the completion of a successful day, a week on track. It bred empowerment. It made me aware of small victories, all the times when I might have once eaten a half-dozen cookies and now was able to stop at one. These were milestones. Between that November and the following January, I lost another 20 pounds.

What I learned in those six months had less to do with food and more to do with myself. It taught me about the nature of struggle and the feeling of strength that's born from it. I look back now and know that the beginning of weight loss—the time just after the first two weeks, when the diet began to feel like a lifestyle—was easier than when the losing slowed. At the start, I was enthusiastic.

Like anything that challenges me, I wanted badly to win. To win at weight loss as fiercely as I might want to win, say, a game of Jeopardy with Daniel.

I squinted to see a 140-pound finish line far off in the distance, and I took off in a mad dash without considering whether I'd run out of fuel halfway or whether the finish line was even as close as it appeared. Thankfully, the first leg of the journey involved weeks of losing double digits since I'd been so big to start with. This experience was something akin to fun but not actually enjoyable, describable only in long, relieved, and accomplished sighs. I felt energetic, then. Inspired.

But then, after I'd been at it for about six months, and was down nearly 60 pounds since my start at 268, I started to slow. In progress, in patience. The vigilance, the exercise—they wore on me. The thrill of newness evaporated, and I began to feel bored with the whole process. I shuddered when reality reminded me, *I hate to be the bearer of bad news, but . . . you're going to have to keep at this for another ten months—give or take forever—if you want to get and keep all that weight off.*

It felt as though I'd been bowling on bumper lanes for a month—knocking pins down, considering myself a boss at the whole game—when all of a sudden the bumpers retreated, and I was left with the real deal, deep, foreboding gutters and all. *This isn't nearly as fun,* I'd think. *I'm not knocking 'em down the way I did before.*

What I thought next—just after I silently called myself a quitter, a loser, all manner of bad names—was simple enough: *Oh, it's just going to suck for a while.*

A heady dose of reality, it was a revelation. Because for once,

I realized that weight loss wouldn't be like taking up jogging as a new hobby, with a map or course directions in hand. It would be like running a marathon, where miles ten through twenty-six just purely, uncompromisingly suck.

Once I said this to myself, much of the journey seemed clearer. I recognized the distance, the real strength that I'd have to maintain. I recognized that I probably wouldn't like it at the beginning. But I knew that, as with many arduous journeys, they often end well.

But there were times, dozens upon dozens, when I seriously wanted a whole box of glazed doughnuts. When I wanted to sit in my bed and eat and eat and eat to my favorite TV shows. When I wanted to attempt eating a whole cake, whether or not my stomach wanted to do it with me. When I didn't want anything to do with willpower or her cousin, moderation. When I didn't want one scoop of ice cream when I knew that Ben & Jerry's offered pints.

There is simply no denying the hard parts. The afternoons when I was midway between lunch and dinner and knew no amount of fruit would ever satisfy like a cupcake. The mornings when I found myself setting the pace on the treadmill and my legs felt leaden, my whole body a heavy mess. Looking at my empty dinner plate after finishing a complete meal and wanting another full one to replace it. The times just before bed when I couldn't sleep because my mind was running the aisles of a supermarket grabbing Oreos and Lucky Charms in a fever. The times in the coffee shop that I smelled a just-baked blueberry muffin and I sighed, realizing I couldn't let myself eat three, hot, and with butter. The times when a sheet cake was splayed in front of me and I knew that "just a sliver" wouldn't cut it.

Those were the trying times. Those were the minutes, the hours, when I needed to brace myself and ride it out. They are the ones that make up character. Because, really, how we act when times are just peachy is nothing compared to how we act when times are rotten. The peachy times don't say as much, anyway, about strength or determination. Moments when I felt my weakest, when I was absolutely certain that I'd rather give up than keep going—that was when I learned what I'm made of.

I developed an arsenal of ways to distract myself, if only to narrowly escape a binge. I wrote in a journal each time I felt myself flagging, in need of support. I called Kate or Sabrina and talked about things other than food and weight and losing. Those conversations let me step outside of my own bubble, to immerse myself in someone else's life. I went to the movies, a place where I had finally learned to be content without snacks, and immersed myself in fantasy worlds. I spent time outside in nature—the surest, quickest way to feel connected to something greater, and a way for me to realize that the world still spun on its axis whether or not I hated my body.

In my moments of deepest despair, when I could no longer avoid the unease building inside me, I would turn to Daniel. He was the only person with whom I was comfortable enough to really address what I was feeling. He'd listen to me cry, always offering a sympathetic ear and a bit of practical, encouraging advice. It brought us closer. As honest as I was with my friends, I couldn't muster the courage to talk as openly with them about how badly I missed the food I once abused; it would seem silly to anyone—strange, even—that I mourned it like I did. Or at least I thought it would. But that shame didn't exist with Daniel, because he, too, struggled with binge eating. He, too, had a lifelong strained relationship to food. He, too, was struggling to lose weight and get healthier. Selfishly, I was grateful for that.

Not every day breezed by. Not every day did my hunger and fullness remain consistent, reliable. Not every day did something stress me out so much that I fought myself to avoid reaching for fudge to fix it. Still, there were those times. And I find it helpful, now, to know this. I find it helpful to know the risks, the challenges that might come up along the way. Because then I know to steel my resolve. I know that we all fight through such moments. That it's just part of the journey.

Just as I began to acknowledge this, just as I began to accept it, I left the country.

7

MOVING TO ITALY WAS PRECARIOUS. Less because of the cultural differences and more because of the expectations involved in spending a semester abroad. "You'll have the best time of your life," everyone assured me. "Enjoy every second," they pressed. *And what if I don't?* I wondered. *What if I find that studying Italian cinema for five months isn't all I've ever wanted and needed in an adventure? Will I be able to sustain my love for a boyfriend who is four thousand miles away? What if I'm not one of those who finds herself while far away on some exotic journey? What will that say about me?*

I feared how the buildup would match its unfolding. And at first I was fine. The first three weeks of the semester were spent in Florence as an orientation period where we would get our feet wet in Italian culture and prepare for the rest of our stay—four months in Rome. There, in Florence, I nearly lost myself in culture lust. It was new and charming and the kind of thing I—or anyone, really—dreamed it would be.

By the time I stepped onto Italian soil, my weight had dropped to 210 pounds. I felt more confident wearing the new clothes I'd packed—a knee-length caramel-colored peacoat, dark-wash trouser jeans in size sixteen, and fitted, crisp white button-down shirts. I continued to count points, flexible yet loyal to Weight Watchers. My aim was to taste everything, at least a bite or two of every last thing. I stuck to small, sensible portions, knowing that most of the food was rich. A handful of pillowy gnocchi, each no bigger than the tip of my thumb; six strands of tender homemade pappardelle pasta in rich Bolognese sauce; grilled eggplant brushed with fruity olive oil; whole branzino with bones to be removed tableside. Dinners out were a sampling of the best Italian fare. It seemed that everyone who ate with us—from teachers to tour guides—was wildly passionate about the food. A meal wasn't complete without at least one person bringing up the special care with which it had been prepared, the freshness of the ingredients. It was infectious, this reverence. And even eating all these things, I still felt on track. I didn't have a scale to help me check in—I didn't even know if Italy housed such a thing—but I could tell that I was doing well despite the decadence.

At the end of the first three weeks in Florence, it was time to move to Rome. Forty of us—all students from various colleges in the United States—filled one bus. In fours, we scattered about the city into our own apartments—everywhere from Trastevere to the less savory area surrounding Termini train station. My loft apartment, to be shared with three girls so wonderful I couldn't have hand-selected them better myself, was in the heart of Campo de' Fiori. Literally "field of flowers," it is a gorgeous square where vendors set up dozens of carts every day to sell fresh fruit, vegetables, and flowers. The space is cobblestoned and quaint, alive with street culture. Old World and unpretentious, beautiful without being styled. Everywhere I'd turn, I would catch mingling aromas of red-sauced pizzette and bitter espresso cutting through the sweet scent of pastries and tarts being pulled from the ovens of *caffès*. Gray-haired signoras wanting nothing more than to feed you, and on every corner Italian men standing with both hands pressed together in front of their chests as if in prayer, shaking them up and down as they barter. At night, Campo turns down its streetlamps and ups the volume of its music to become a party scene for Italians and tourists alike.

The whole place seemed almost like a storybook world.

But that first night in Rome, a sprawling metropolis, uprooted from the village that I knew Florence to be, I felt homesick. Transition within transition, I was emotionally taxed. It made me sad and, worse, lonely. I tried to call Daniel with the international calling card I'd picked up at the airport, but when I was met by his voice mail, the loneliness ached deeper.

After setting my belongings down in my new apartment, I hit the corner market to buy necessities for a yet-to-be-filled fridge: eggs (unrefrigerated, mind you), greens for salad, fruit, milk (also unrefrigerated), cereal. I browsed the aisles, comparing home and here, trying my best to read labels in a language I'd only studied for a semester. Nutrition facts, euros, ingredient laundry lists— all a foreign affair in my effort to stay the healthy course abroad. I pushed my cart to the front to pay and paused. At the register, American candy bars smiled at me, sweet and familiar. *Kit Kat, there you are.* I sighed, relieved to see a piece of home. Chocolate-covered and cooing at me. I picked up the package, a bag of Kit Kat

Pop 'Em Bites. I imagine it served five in a reasonable world, but one in mine. My heartbeat quickened. Close to a choice I should not be making, I felt excited and anxious, on the ledge of jumping into food oblivion. The decision made itself. Into the cart the Kit Kats went. That was it, I realized; I had decided to binge. Too late to turn back now, I swiveled that clunky cart back to face the aisles. *There was that one section*, I thought as I headed to it. Before me, parallel shelves stood proud to show their full stock of cookies and crunchies and all manner of sweet-meets-sweeter. Paranoid, I looked to my left and right, wanting to be sure that no one had caught me almost cheating on health with floozy snacks containing more calories than a mug of heavy cream, straight up. *Want. Need. Crave and love and long and lust.* I salivated. I felt manic and depressive. *Don't. Do. Don't. Do. Don't. Do. Do Not. Do.*

I snatched the vanilla creme wafers—the family pack—swiftly and surely and tucked them into the corner of my cart. *The cashier won't think anything of two sweet treats, will she?* I made sure to stagger the contents within the cart—vegetable, Kit Kat, fruit, milk, sugar wafers, eggs—all in an effort to not look like a two-hundred-something-pound girl on the verge of a desperate binge.

Once you've decided on a binge, it's almost impossible to stop. Turning back is driving all the way to Florida from Massachusetts, straight through the night, and arriving bleary-eyed and exhausted, only to decide it would be better to turn around and head back up north rather than nap in the sun on the beach for a bit. It's starving for days, only to enter a buffet line with no plate, no fork, no knife, no spoon. You consider using your hands, no matter how barbaric, how publicly embarrassing. It hardly feels doable to go back on what you've just decided will be a swan dive into pleasure.

As I handed a fistful of euros to the cashier, I realized I already felt better. Something about having the Kit Kats, the sugar wafers in my possession soothed me. I breathed easier, knowing sweet relief would come after only a short walk back to my apartment.

There was hardly enough space in that little fridge to fit four girls' worth of groceries. I left the kitchen with the chocolate and cookies and returned to my new bedroom, closing the door behind me. My roommate, Melissa, was there unzipping her suitcase. Her eyes showed homesickness, the same strain as mine. I set my suitcase atop my twin bed, ripped open its top, and did the same with the Kit Kat package. I showed her the snacks by splaying them out before her as an offering. She had seen me eat healthfully during the previous three weeks, so this splurge was unexpected. When she made mention of the indulgence, I felt backed into a corner with nothing to say but the truth. I told her how much I was struggling—with a new city, a new body. I told her how much weight I'd lost, how hard and rewarding the last six months had been, and how badly I wanted to take a break from it all and eat chocolate. She gave me a sympathetic nod, pulling a handful of Kit Kat bites from the bag on my bed and popping two into her mouth. "Well, these would have been my choice, too." She smiled as she chewed. "And I think you'll be okay."

I tossed a chocolate into my mouth. I felt a relief not unlike submerging myself in a swimming pool after lying for hours in the unrelenting sun. Sure enough, I was comforted the whole time I ate them. Melissa and I went about unpacking, and I continued eating all the while. When the Kit Kat bag could be upturned without a chocolatey crumb left, I started in on the sugar wafers. I ate until I felt sick. But I didn't, I couldn't, stop.

Later, after I'd mildly recovered from extreme fullness, Melissa and I walked to a pizzeria I'd passed on my way into the city. There I placed an order for four *arancini*—deep-fried balls of risotto—and a huge slice of pepperoni pizza. Melissa ate a meal half that size and didn't say anything about the enormity of my appetite.

I ate, perhaps without even tasting any of it, trying to keep up a conversation when all I could think of was the food. The guilt set in as I trudged the two flights up to our apartment. I sincerely wished I could take it all back—the candy, the wafers, the *arancini*, the pizza. None of it felt worth the setback in my weight loss progress. *Two steps forward, one step back*, I reprimanded myself.

I showered, as if to shampoo the shame away. The hot water wrapped around me in a hug. When I slipped between the covers of my twin bed that night, I switched on the tiny book light I'd brought with me and wrote in my journal. It was the first time I'd written about the emotional side of the journey, rather than simply penning my usual notes on what I'd eaten. I started with a couple of paragraphs about my food infidelity. How I'd cheated on health and myself with cheap thrills like chocolate and pizza. What started as a guilt-ridden rant against my binge turned right and left down roads that revealed my real anxiety and homesickness. Three furiously written pages in, I realized I wasn't writing about food at all any longer. I was writing about how the change of setting from Florence to Rome had rattled me, made me feel bewildered and alone. I noticed myself doing what I so often did in the past: I began to paint it black. I took the single smudge on an otherwise beautiful painting, and I smeared it more. I let the mistake bleed all over, in thick brushstrokes of regret. Covered what was once good and unique with a film of black. Tears rose. *Don't do this, Andie.* I pressed closed the leather journal and switched off the light, too tired to fight myself any longer.

The problem with bingeing was that although I promised myself I would not do it again, I silently wished I could. On the one hand, I wanted to be right back on track, doing well and paying attention to what I was eating; and on the other, I wanted to veer off course and stay riding in the direction that wound into oblivion. It was this dichotomy that killed me. The wanting to be different in order to be perceived as better, yet wishing I didn't have to try so hard.

I wished I could find some hideaway, somewhere I could be as reclusive as I pleased and just eat. And eat. And cry. And eat. And cry. I wondered, momentarily, if maybe I'd had the right idea in the beginning of high school, when I'd silently resigned myself to being the fat girl. *Should I go back to that? Was it easier then?* I thought fondly back to the days when I'd stopped caring.

When I woke the next morning, I opened my eyes to a stream of sunlight breaking through the curtains. Before I could soak in a full twenty serene seconds, I remembered all that I'd gorged on. Getting off the bed, I felt that fat, guilty brick in my stomach, and I wished it were possible to grab it, rip it out of my body, and throw it as far as my arm strength would allow.

I thought about writing the whole day off as ruined and promising to start anew tomorrow, the way I'd done in the past. In seconds I had a mental list that began and ended with gelato—all that I'd plow through if I were to go through with a spoiled day turned binge. I dabbled in the sweet possibility that the gelateria up the road had a "Gotta Have It" size like Cold Stone Creamery back home. I paused. It would have been easy. But I realized that

I couldn't knowingly look to food for a way out when it had so clearly led me here. It wasn't hunger that beckoned me to eat more. It wasn't my stomach that needed to be reconciled. It was shame. It was guilt. And food can't remedy such things.

I dressed and walked ten minutes past the Tiber River to Trastevere, the nook of Rome where Google had promised me I'd find a gym. It was all I could do to distract myself from creeping thoughts of cannoli. Up two flights to a small apartment, I immediately realized that the Italian version of gym wasn't in line with the American one. The space seemed filtered in that grainy, old-timey-photo haze, with the same dated effect as the pictures in Mom's childhood album. Everything tinted yellow, blown out, and overexposed—dusty, almost. This four-room flat with two rickety old treadmills, two '70s-style free-weight sets, wrought iron weight benches, dingy foam mats, and the strongest smell of salty-sweat-meets-my-nana's-musty-basement was nothing I'd ever experienced before. In each room, an aging Italian man stood perspiring in a ribbed white tank top, light heather-gray sweatpants with elastic banding around his ankles, and a terry cloth sweatband rounding his full head of hair. I thought of my grandfather, all potbellied and purposeful, doing his daily set of ten push-ups in the living room.

Smiling warmly at the gentleman behind the front desk—quite literally a student's desk; there was no formal entryway whatsoever—I told him my name and asked him, in Italian gibberish, for a membership.

I left the so-called gym and stepped back out into a sunny day. Regardless of how poor an establishment it was, I knew I needed it. I continued walking through Trastevere in no particular direction. Already, the guilt of the night before had begun to fade.

The following morning, I returned to the gym, a brief jaunt from Campo alongside the Tiber and across Ponte Sisto. Just the sight of the treadmill in that small back room petrified me. I had never been successful at running consistently in my life, especially that one time I attempted the mile at lacrosse tryouts and, upon completion, promptly threw up. *Let's give this another go,* I thought as I stepped up onto the better of the two treadmills—the one that shook a fraction less violently when moving. I had to try running, anyhow; there weren't any other cardio machines. Headphones positioned firmly on my ears, I pressed Start. I jogged for a while, and then, sure that I'd completed fifteen minutes, I looked down to find I'd only run for six.

I want to quit, I want to quit, I want to quit. And when I'm done quitting, I'd like to quit again.

I plodded on, determined to see the red digital timer reach twenty minutes. My lungs neared explosion, burning so intensely I was sure they'd catch fire any second. My belly bounced. I swore aloud and then glanced to my right and left, not wanting to have offended anyone. I spent the remaining eternity on the treadmill wishing it to be over. When I realized that time did not speed up in direct connection to my rising resentment for running, I made promises to myself that it would get easier.

Over the course of three weeks, somehow, some way, it did. I built up to a steady jog—one in which I wouldn't need to stop more than twice. At five miles per hour, for thirty solid minutes, I carried all two-hundred-some-odd pounds of me. The sense of accomplishment that tingled through me as I'd finish each morning almost dulled the soreness in my quads, my butt, my calves.

After my film classes let out in the afternoons, I walked around the city. Sometimes purposefully and sometimes not, but usually with Melissa. All that mattered to the two of us was that we explored, that we saw every part of Rome. Every monument, every antique church, every centuries-old piazza. And I was glad to have endless destinations, reasons to keep moving. I took the stairs when there were escalators available; I walked to class when there were buses; I traveled to Naples and climbed Mount Vesuvius with new friends I'd made on a rainy Tuesday morning, when my unbalanced self would have been better suited to sitting at its base.

And there, in a city, a country, that doesn't necessarily believe in formal exercise, I learned to run. If I close my eyes tight, I can almost still feel the up and down jiggling of a body with essentially three filled backpacks of excess strapped to it. The way pants always loved giving me wedgies. The raw patches made from chafing.

Every day, every run, every walk was triumphant. I was getting there. Even without a scale to offer proof, I knew I was losing. I knew that I was changing. But if I wasn't able to identify my birthmarks while staring at my own jiggly body each evening, I wouldn't have believed the person I'd become. I wouldn't have known whose body I was looking at. The size sixteen trouser jeans I'd bought just before coming to Italy required a tight belt to keep them on my hips. Even the belt needed new holes punched in it to make it smaller.

Three months in, I saw the way I'd transformed when I chose to jog on cobblestones that led past the Roman Forum to the Colosseum. When Melissa and I took our first Bikram yoga class next to St. Peter's Basilica. When I didn't curse more than twice while doing two sets of twenty-six yoga poses in Italian.

Exercise was changing not only my shape, but my relationship with eating, too. I recognized that when I felt better physically, I was more motivated to eat well. The thought of potentially undoing any of the hard work I'd put into walking and running weakened the appeal of bingeing. It became increasingly easier to choose healthy, wholesome foods and to keep my portions of rich, indulgent foods small. For the first time in my life, I was able to eat decadently without gorging. Pasta, bread, pastries, ice cream—all could be eaten within reason.

One weekend, I traveled to Bologna with the close girlfriends I'd made. There, at a *caffè* on some side street, I savored a meal I will never forget.

A carafe of deep ruby wine, the house *vino rosso*, was poured into each of our glasses by the waiter. My first sip was a burst of juicy sweet grapes. I pulled a hunk off the crusty loaf of bread sitting center stage at our table. Slowly I broke it into smaller pieces and dipped each gently into the tiny plate of olive oil, the edges of the bread sopping up the fruity clean flavor. Antipasti came next—a platter of grilled zucchini, eggplant, and asparagus alongside aged cheeses, plump vinaigrette-marinated white beans, and salty olives. A taste of each was enough to whet my appetite. I sat quietly, patiently, waiting for my next course. The time passed slowly, and our conversation meandered through every avenue. Now and again, I glanced around the ten-table *ristorante* at other diners. I envisioned the life of each patron. *They've just fallen in love*, I assumed, staring at the table to my left. *He forgot her birthday*, at my right.

And just as these make-believe tales reached new levels of absurdity, a plate swooped under my nose and settled down in front of me. Tortelloni Bolognese, the specialty of the house. Handmade pasta—plump and bulging with a filling of luscious ricotta and spinach—lay delicately in my shallow dish. Seven of them, altogether. On top, a thick meat sauce steamed my face as I leaned in to breathe the richness of minced beef and veal. The beauty of it—even just the smell alone—was enough to make my mouth water. I stabbed my fork tines through one of the tight crescents of pasta, piercing clean through the silky center. I scooped downward, catching crumbles of tender beef and veal that had simmered low and slow all day. Salt and fat and savory all at once. I felt present, in rapture with such deliciousness. Seeing only one plump shape left amid a puddle of sauce, I sensed contentment coursing through me. It was what it was: a much-loved meal. *And now,* I said to myself, *it's over. Remember it.* Another plate wouldn't have brought me any greater satisfaction, because contentment doesn't double by the serving.

I walked away from that mahogany table with a fullness of mind. As we left the restaurant, I turned to Melissa as she sighed, wishing every meal could be that good. I didn't say it then, but what I thought was, *Maybe every meal could, if I let it. Maybe the difference between a standard meal and a great meal has as much to do with its taste as it does my perception, my energy in devouring it.* And that was the difference in me. The change I'd undergone—from someone who ate to capacity to distract her mind, into someone who purposely tasted every morsel—was not unconscious. It was a transformation that had taken deliberate effort before and after that meal. I put my fork down between bites instead of making like a shovel and digging in. I let a forkful of food sit on my tongue in order to observe its flavor, to savor it. I paused often during the meal to check in with my hunger and fullness.

Daily, I recommitted to practicing moderation. I'd scramble two eggs and eat them alongside fresh fruit at my apartment for breakfast. I'd find a small *caffè* where I could sit outside and eat a salad for lunch—usually mixed baby greens with balls of fresh mozzarella cheese, tuna, a few glugs of olive oil, and a squeeze of lemon. And in the evening, I'd revel in seeking out a dish or restaurant I hadn't tried before. I'd drink the aged wine spouting from wooden barrels on my street corner. On sunny afternoons, I'd walk the streets on self-guided gelato tastings. The teeny-tiny spoons would help to pace me. They forced small and deliberate licks of *stracciatella* and *nocciola*. And I didn't gorge as I once would have been tempted to. Eating there was different from anything I'd ever experienced. The portions were smaller, and the plates, too. The elegance of a meal wasn't in the food alone, but in the way I'd linger at the table, the way I'd sit for nearly half a night outside at a wrought iron table to people-watch and sip espresso. There was a meaningful nature to eating. It was celebrated; it was an activity done three times per day. No more. No less.

The food had not changed. It had not become tastier, more flavor packed since I arrived in Italy in January. My appreciation of it had. I focused my desires on reveling in moderation, and the urges to binge fell away, slowly, over time. Of course, there remained certain foods—all things sweet, in particular—that begged me to overindulge. Anything cake or pastry. These sweets required a special kind of treatment. I had to start by completely avoiding them so as not to binge, and then I had to learn—painfully slowly—that two pastries never really felt better than one. That the only difference between the enjoyment of three desserts versus one is a higher cost in dollar bills and pride. This was one of my hardest lessons. Because no matter how logically I understood my need to practice moderation, I still craved the feeling of limitlessness.

During the week, I attended classes and film viewings,

acquainting myself with the work of Visconti, Fellini, and Zeffire-
lli. Weekends I'd travel by myself or with friends who were willing
to pay thirty dollars for a turbulent Ryanair flight and an unsavory
hostel stay in a new city: Dublin, Paris, Valencia, Barcelona, Am-
sterdam, London, eleven romantic cities in Italy. The more places
I visited, the more my wanderlust grew. I was starting to feel free.

Near the end of my stay in Rome, my food budget had dwindled. It
made sense, given all the restaurants I'd sampled and the small fortune I spent on calling cards to call Daniel. Melissa and I decided
to make more of our meals at home. The open-air markets—the
fruit and vegetable stands lining Campo—became daily stops on
my way home from classes. In our little kitchen, I began cooking.
I sautéed a mass of vegetables; I dressed arugula in floral olive oil
and a drizzle of sweet balsamic vinegar as thick and ebony as molasses; I tore nubs off a softball of freshly pulled mozzarella and
ate it with bright, fragrant leaves of basil; I boiled strands of angel
hair pasta al dente and, upon draining it, quickly stirred in a scoop
of mascarpone cheese and a fresh egg while the pasta was piping
hot, the heat barely cooking the runny egg. After plating, I'd shred
bits of smoked salmon on top, adding a welcome salty contrast to
the creamy pasta. It was my own version of carbonara. And late at
night, when Melissa and I watched episode after episode of *Grey's
Anatomy* on her laptop, we'd munch popcorn we had made on the
stove top: a thin coating of olive oil at the bottom of a large pot
followed by a handful of popcorn kernels. We shook salt, garlic
powder, and Parmesan cheese into the hot pot and shook the corn
around until each kernel was lightly coated in the sharp garlic-and-
cheese mixture. It felt fun, like the old days of digging into Fritos

bags while watching *Dawson's Creek* with Sabrina. I could still have the illusion of snacking, volume- and flavorwise, while keeping my intake within the point range I'd learned at Weight Watchers, using my own wonky estimation system without any formal calculator.

I left Rome in mid-May with a heavy heart.

But I stepped off the plane a new girl.

There, in baggage claim, was Mom, with tears just streaming down her milky-white Irish cheeks. She snatched me toward her and held me as though I might fly away again if not somehow anchored to her. She tucked her nose into my neck and breathed my hair. "My baby. I missed you," she said.

Pulling back to look at her, I smiled, "Me too, Mumma."

Our love spell broke with Mom practically shouting about my changed body, each word spoken in staccato for greater effect. She held me out in front of her at arm's length, as if assessing wall art. "Oh, my God! Look at you!" Again with the tears.

Leaving the airport, I saw my reflection in the clear glass panel of windows. *Whose body is this?* was the only thought racing through my mind. Tall and slender and . . . *normal.*

I grinned at my reflection, as broadly as ever, near giddy at what I'd accomplished. I met eyes with a woman walking out beside us. She stared at my crazy-eyed smile. Amused, she asked in a slightly patronizing tone, "Happy?!"

I looked at her, embarrassed by my odd behavior.

"Very." I smiled brightly at her as I turned away.

I could barely contain the joy. I knew it even before I stepped on the scale and saw that I had lost 55 pounds. I felt proud, alive. I was twenty-one now and, for the first time, appropriately weighed in for my height at 155 pounds. My jeans hung low on my hips, still the size fourteens Mom had mailed me midway through my trip when I told her that the sixteens and eighteens I had brought with me were too big. The one thin belt I'd packed did its best to keep them up, but it created a large gap at my waist, the pants folding in on themselves and falling below the belt's line. *I wonder what size I should be wearing now?* I asked myself.

I went to UMass to visit Daniel during his last week of the semester. He knew how much weight I'd lost, and I knew how hard he'd struggled to do the same despite all our old temptations. It had been nearly six months since we'd seen each other last. I waited outside his dorm, hoping someone would exit the locked building so that I could slip in before the door swung shut. I did manage to sneak in—I wanted to knock on the door to his room, to reveal myself as he opened it. It seemed more personal than meeting outside. As he opened the door, a look of utter surprise enveloped his face. It was clear that he'd lost weight—perhaps another thirty pounds. He looked healthier. His face was thinner; his clothes hung looser. Reaching out, he pulled me into him, not saying a word for the first moments that he held me. I remembered the strength and familiarity of him. Our bodies were closer in that embrace than I could remember them being before. Without my belly as a barrier, his arms wrapped fully around me. "You're so small!" It felt good to hear him say that, since he knew how much I'd struggled to reach that size. Raising his hands to hold the sides of my face, he kissed me.

There were days during the first weeks of being home when I just wanted to be out and about. I wanted to do all the things I hadn't done before with any measure of grace. I crossed my legs casually, coolly; I walked even more. I bought new clothing in sizes like eight and, unbelievably, six. I discovered how much cheaper it was to be thin—the way clearance racks practically shout your name, since they're loaded with smaller sizes. I found pacing the mall insanely fun. Browsing, trying on clothes just because; it was exhilarating to pick an outfit—any outfit—and know that, at the very least, it would look okay. Not necessarily perfect for me, but decent. I began emerging from behind the curtains and walking barefoot to the tri-fold mirror at the center of the dressing rooms, an act I had detested before. Now I fit better into everything. Shirts, pants, dresses, life.

When June arrived, I rejoined that old YMCA where I'd spent the previous summer with Kate. In no time, we were at it again: taking aerobics classes with the rowdiest of fifty-year-olds, Jazzercising, being debaucherous with exercise balls and an open weight room. And laughing. Laughing so much.

I'd almost call it fun, if the range for experiencing fun were a ladder on which the bottom rung was still kind of adjacent to low-level torture. The whole process of losing weight was easier now, a year in. I was used to the meals I prepared, the way I moved my body to the point of profuse sweating day in and day out. I still faced a sense of dread before some workouts, and, naturally, I still lusted after cake, but at least I was getting there. Envisioning myself at the goal I'd set for myself—140 pounds—was easier. Mere miles from the finish line of my marathon, I broke into a sprint.

I lost another 22 pounds over those next two months. And on the final day of summer, just as I was saying good-bye to Kate and the Y, and heading back to UMass for senior year, I saw a number I didn't think I'd ever see: 133.

On our first day back, Daniel, Sabrina, Nicole, and I drove to campus from our newly rented apartment and walked to our film class. The stares were unnerving. *Is my fly unzipped?* I looked down to check. My eyes met those of others walking past us. Each seemed more aware of me than I'd known people to be before. With guys and girls alike, I felt more accepted, respected. Not simply thin, but valued. Desirable.

People I'd known since freshman year—who'd come to know me big—were stunned. Mouths hung gaping as they took in such a transformation. I was applauded and admired. And Daniel, who loved me all the way through, looked so proud when guy friends of ours would smile from me to him and whisper, "You are unbelievably lucky, man." I knew from the way he nodded and looked at me that he'd love me regardless. Daniel himself had lost weight—a total of 75 pounds since the previous fall—and I admired his dedication. He seemed to gain more confidence. Now at 225 pounds, he looked better than ever.

It was thrilling going out in Amherst. Nights at bars, parties, even just walking through campus to class—it was all exhilarating. For the very first time, I was exactly the girl I'd always wanted to be.

Those first few months when I inhabited a new, hard-earned body were a raw, explosive high. A high unlike any other experience I'd had.

But after all highs comes a low.

8

I LOOKED INTO THE MIRROR AND LOVED WHAT I SAW so completely that all I wanted was to snap a picture of the girl within the frame. I wanted to replace the default picture I held of myself in my head—that of the fat girl I'd always been—with the new one. Swap out fat for thin. I scanned my body, gave myself the kind of admiring up-and-down eye that few guys had ever given me. I saw a jawline. Collarbones, two pronounced collarbones. And both were mine. A waist. *A waist.* I found my knees and, with them, an understanding why anyone might refer to knees as knobby. Staring at my body, pinching my love handles, I struggled to absorb that these changes were real. I wanted to stay this way.

Without that mirror, without any way of physically seeing my own form in plain sight, I still believed myself to be the fat girl. My mind and eyes were in opposition.

A part of me was disdainful of the newfound attention I was receiving. *You see me now? I'm attractive now?* Receiving the congratulations, the praises in some small way felt like accepting that what I'd been before—all of my life—was wrong. Even though I'd often felt that way myself, I resented that the size of my body was correlated to my value, my worth as a person. The praise was a confirmation that thinness made me the better version of myself. And since something about it still felt foreign and unnatural to me, the outside praise made my insides cower. *I'm not ready for this,* I'd think. *I'm not better now just because of this body. I don't even know how to stay here. What if I can't stay here? If I gain it all back?* In a way, it all felt like a trap. Before, when I was fat, no one spoke aloud about my body. They couldn't. There's no decent way to bring up someone's obesity. And now the thinness was the centerpiece on the table of conversation. It was out there, aired and allowed to be its own entity. Something we could point at and discuss.

With all the compliments I received for my weight loss, I feared returning to fat. An intense anxiety settled into my bones. I felt pressure. This was different from striving to do well in school, wanting to please Mom, wanting to fit in. *They're watching me now.* Unhelpfully, a friend of the family reminded me, "You know, Andrea, losing weight is the easy part. It's maintaining it that's really hard." This sentiment made me seethe. *How dare anyone minimize that struggle, that agonizing journey of losing weight?* I was shocked that they'd deem losing 135 pounds "easy" and, worse, that they'd want to instill a fear in me about keeping it off. Of course losing weight wasn't easy. Ten pounds, 20, 50, 100-plus—any amount is challenging. It all requires discipline and an absolute desire to change. Losing necessitates feeling terrible now so that you can feel better later. I thought back to the days when I cried desperately, almost giving up on losing weight altogether. I remembered the writhing, the feeling of hopelessness and withdrawal of coming down from twenty years of food addiction. Perhaps those people simply wanted to remind me that the journey wasn't over, that maintenance involved the same vigilance over what I ate as losing did. But I hated to hear the work diminished, relegated to ordinary. *Yes, I get it*, I wanted to tell them. *It looks like I've just moved into a new home, a very desirable and thin one, and now you're reminding me that I have to come up with the mortgage payments. I'm terrified, too. But just so you know, I worked to purchase this house myself, and somehow I'll figure it out.*

What worried me almost as much as letting myself down if I gained it all back, was letting everyone else down. Being a failure. The pressure, the foreignness of it all caused the welling up of a deep, deep insecurity.

The months that followed—in fact, that whole year—were dark. I was scared all the time. I felt as though the tips of my fingers were moments from losing their death grip on the cliff I clung to. Life wasn't what I'd thought it would be. This wasn't the light and free, casual and content life I'd expected to start.

I had known that losing weight would be difficult. For the thirteen months that I doggedly pursued a smaller self, I promised myself that one day it would all be over. I was certain that with thinness came release, relief. I imagined happiness just behind it. I expected all the hard work I'd put into losing to be rewarded. I imagined that the journey, long and arduous as it was, would lead me to some peaceful paradise. I'd finally be able to shed the backpack that burdened me, every last pound, and I'd sit in ease. There contentment would just seep into my skin like humidity in the air.

I was the smallest I'd ever been. For the first time in my entire twenty-one years of life, I was not obese. I should have been rejoicing in such an accomplishment. The world was supposed to be my oyster. I suppose I thought I would wake up on the morning of my first day in a new body, and life would exist in Day-Glo. Neons, brights, music booming and boisterous, faces smiling, doors unlocked and opening, a fan blowing on me like the ones you see in photo shoots, a sense of purpose, a lightness of spirit.

Instead, it was rain. It was nothing like I'd imagined. The sadness, the isolation, the loneliness, the dullness in color palette. The heaviness of being.

My thoughts were consumed by food. What I'd eat, when I'd eat, how I'd eat, and how much it all cost nutritionally filled the entirety of my brain space. I found it hard to focus on anything else. I became obsessed not only with counting calories and trying to stay at the exact same number each day, but with the healthfulness of the foods I consumed, too. I'd enter a grocery store and browse for sixty minutes, internally screaming at myself for not being able to even choose what I wanted. I couldn't manage the decision between what was healthiest, what sounded best at the moment, and what I could "afford" in my calorie budget. All I wanted was to eat alone, in quiet, in secret. I needed to avoid eyes, speculation, and judgment of what I'd chosen to put on my plate. Damned if I did, damned if I didn't—I felt as though everything I ate in view of others was wrong. A salad made them think I lived in a cage of diet and restriction. "How boring it must be to eat only lettuce," or "Salad's for the birds," and "Maybe that's why I'm not thin . . . I can't give up taste just to be skinny!" Or if the salad was big, voluminous but certainly lower in calories than, say, a sandwich or soup, people would comment on its enormity. "Wow, that's huge!

I can't believe you weigh less than I do and you eat so much!" Or they'd remark on the fruits and vegetables I chose, warning me of all the gobs of sugar in pineapple and the loads of fat in avocado. Both are perfectly healthy but come with misperceptions of their nutritious virtue. And if I dared have a slice of pizza—alongside a salad, no doubt—they looked at me with worried eyes. "Careful. You don't want to put that weight back on." Nothing I put into my mouth went without comment by someone. I imagined myself under a microscope, with everyone gathering closely to see what I'd do next. I begged silently to be left alone. Paranoia set in and, with it, a greater need for compulsive control.

Save for Daniel, I felt isolated. I told him every last detail of my unraveling. I let him into the obsessive downward spiral of my new world. His support, his unrelenting belief that "it will get better, kiddo" held me together just enough that I wasn't falling apart. He stayed home with me when I couldn't bear to be out. He was patient. He tiptoed while I stomped, whispered while I screamed. But the comfort wasn't without its own set of problems. Pouring my inner turmoil onto him left me empty and him drowning. There wasn't room for him when our home of a relationship was filled to the hilt with me and me and me. As I began to feel guilty, I started retreating from even him, my sole source of peace.

I still missed eating the foods I'd shunned while losing. The gooey cookies, the cupcakes, every single candy bar—I hated the part of me that wanted them badly. I dismissed her as weak. My body felt as rigid, as tight, as my whole life had become. And while my weight hadn't dipped to an unnatural low, my mind had.

I felt myself withdrawing, and my friends, my family, they saw it, too. I began staying home more, not wanting, not even feeling able, to stray from routine. Being social was exhausting, as though it were taking something out of me, an energy I didn't have in the first place. I made excuses to stay at home on Fridays, on Saturdays. What I tried to display as a natural decline in my desire to go out partying was a cover for my fear of the calories that came with drinking and late-night eating. I couldn't save up enough calories in the day to waste on alcohol; they were far too precious to be used frivolously. I couldn't bear the thought of how hungry I might be after a night at the bars, when we'd return home and everyone suggested takeout pizza and calzones. I would not, could not, commit to coffee dates, mall trips, movies, anything before I'd completed my workout for the day.

I weighed and measured every morsel, never straying from my allowance of sixteen hundred calories a day. I panicked at restaurants when I was out of my own kitchenly control.

One Friday night, after a week of convincing on Daniel's part and careful deliberation on mine, we ventured out to dinner and a movie. We went to the Amherst Brewing Company, an old favorite of ours, where I had never missed an opportunity to order one of their specialty build-your-own burgers and sweet potato fries. Daniel was hopeful that being in a spot we once loved would remind me of the fun we used to have, when dates were casual and eating was easy.

The moment we were seated, I felt a cold sweat break out all over me, like hives. The menu. The options. The decisions. The hidden calories. What I wanted. What I should want. *How much oil? Is that a fancy way of saying fried?* I was lost. Daniel reached across the table and put his hand on mine, smiling and reassuring me. "Please, get whatever you want most. One meal won't do any harm." I looked at him and nodded, not believing a word of it. I was grateful that he chose to eat healthy with me most of the time. But he struggled with consistency, often limboing between either eating restrictively or bingeing. The weight he'd lost over the summer and the semester before was slowly starting to creep back on.

"I think I'm going to get this salad," I offered. His face dropped slightly, as if he'd anticipated handmade pasta and instead got packaged ramen noodles. He urged me to reconsider, to order exactly what sounded most delicious to me in that moment. Trying to fight against the obsessive voice in my head, I did.

I ordered the meatloaf. And then, instead of enjoying our date, I agonized over my choice all the minutes before our meals arrived. We barely held on to the thread of a conversation, because I couldn't concentrate on Daniel. My mind raced around like crazy, regretting the meatloaf.

"Can we cancel it?" I asked him.

"Just try it," he said softly.

I saw our waitress walking toward us with two solid platters weighing down both of her hands. When she set mine down in front of me, the smells of seasoned beef and buttery mashed potatoes hit me hard. Hunger, desire—they came to me like old memories. I wanted them.

Just as I began to give in, my new form of obsession sounded off like an alarm in my head. It shattered my reverie. In seconds, I pushed my plate away from me. It was as if the control system in my brain had sent out emergency signals. I wanted no part of that plate. I wanted to leave.

The hour that followed is a memory that exists with such a halo of shame that I have tried to block it out. On Daniel's urging, I rigidly ate half of that meatloaf and a quarter of the potatoes. I chewed each bite hatefully, painfully, as though even enjoyment would add extra calories. Outwardly, I was angry at him. For wanting me to eat it when he knew how much I struggled, for urging me to order it in the first place. But inwardly, I was angry with myself for allowing my obsession to ruin not only our date, but my life, too.

Finally, I threw my napkin over my plate and walked out of the restaurant. Daniel quickly paid the bill, not having eaten more than half of his pulled pork, and rushed out to catch me. We drove home in a car filled with the shrill sounds of my hysteria. Sobbing, I shouted the most brutal, hurtful things I could muster in my mind at Daniel. He argued back, the volume of his voice gradually rising. Over and over, he tried to get me to see that the meal wasn't nearly the big deal I was making it. But I couldn't believe that I'd eaten all I had. How many calories had I consumed? I hated him for the whole meal. It was his idea, after all. I wished, desperately, to erase the entire night, to wipe clean the slate of my calories as if they were scribbles on a chalkboard.

When we got inside our apartment, I'd reached a breaking point. Daniel wasn't acknowledging how much the meal had affected me, or at least he wasn't willing to accept it. In no time, it became a fight about our whole relationship and not simply the meatloaf I'd eaten. Every wrongdoing, every past hurt, everything faulty between the two of us was dredged up. And when I couldn't handle the mounting discomfort inside me any longer, I slapped him across the face.

I then collapsed against him in hysteria, simultaneously seeking support and lashing out in pathetic violence. He swallowed me in his embrace, holding me tightly, offering comfort and protecting himself from my flailing limbs.

I slapped him because I couldn't slap myself as easily. I slapped him because I couldn't contain the rage coursing through my veins. I slapped him so he would feel pain, the way I did. I slapped him because of my own cowardice, because of my inability to accept my own actions. I slapped him because of meatloaf. And even a thousand apologies will never change it. I slapped him.

The next day, I found myself sitting in a corner of Daniel's and my bedroom, feeling a kind of hopelessness that I'd never known before. There weren't enough apologies to give to Daniel. Regret spilled from my eyes. I recognized the cold, hard floor as what it was: rock bottom.

Daniel urged me to seek help—a nutritionist, a therapist, anyone who could help. His suggestion didn't make me defensive. I knew the love and concern that informed it. Together we searched online for nutritionists. I called the first one that popped up in my Google results.

Three days later, I had my first visit with a registered dietitian. I told her my history—the whole long journey from there to here. And when I was done, she paused to think a minute before speaking.

"You know, Andie, many people can think of at least one time in their lives when they felt at ease with food, or at least that they had an appropriate relationship with it at some point. They probably didn't have to think too hard about what they'd eat and how it would fuel them; they just had a trust in themselves and their hunger and fullness cues. Children are excellent examples of having a natural food intuition. They eat when they are hungry and generally stop when they are full. But you have never had what one can consider a 'normal' relationship with food. For you, it seems the earliest memories involve overeating or eating for some other reason than hunger. So, then, I cannot tell you to return to a place of trust with food, a state of normal eating. You have to learn that now at twenty-one."

She made sense. Perhaps walking in the door that morning, I'd assumed she would give me a meal plan, something prescriptive to help usher out the anxiety. I thought she'd tell me to eat more, or I at least wished that she'd tell me something that concrete. What she gave me instead was a frame of mind, a clue that the work would be much more than what to eat and when. It involved changing how my mind worked. She encouraged me to think less about the food itself and more about the ways I was using it as something other than physical nourishment. An hour into our session, she sensed how broken I was.

And then she told me, almost apologetically, "We're going to get through this. But, my dear, you've developed a form of eating disorder. Not traditional anorexia or bulimia, no. But your intense fears, your preoccupations and current obsessive thought patterns are in line with EDNOS, which stands for 'Eating Disorder Not Otherwise Specified.'" Her eyes scanned my face, the expression in hers soft and compassionate.

Hearing her describe the category of disorder, I realized that all of my life was an eating disorder. No one who reaches morbid obesity is without a disorder of eating. No one whose weight preoccupies their lives for two decades. Only now, I'd swung sharply from a lifetime of overeating to extreme restriction. Both sides of the same obsessive coin.

She suggested I see a therapist. I was apprehensive about the idea at first. Not because I thought therapy was only for the deranged, the semi-screwed-up, but because I worried, *Can it even help me?* I was certain that I was beyond therapy. *There's nothing I haven't openly admitted to myself, nothing I don't already know about myself.* I thought of Mom, who had gone to the same counselor for years and never seemed to find any relief for her aching mind.

And yet I went anyway. It was desperation that practically escorted me through the office door. *Save me,* I thought upon seeing the therapist's kind face.

I wish I could say that the therapy saved me, but it did not. It simply could not. Nothing on its own could fix everything. But the talking aloud helped. Being forced to verbalize my feelings and anxieties changed a part of me at least. I realized that so much of what I thought about myself and about life in general was slightly askew. My perceptions and the things that seemed truest proved false many times. She suggested journaling, simply putting pen to paper all the times I felt anxious about food—anytime I found myself wanting to tear into three king-size Reese's peanut butter cups while also wishing that Reese's went out of business. *Why are you so uncomfortable in this moment? What is it that makes you want to dive into a chocolate fountain?*

The writing was familiar. Not because I felt I was penning some important piece, but because it forced an articulation of feelings. I wrote in a black Moleskine notebook, mostly at night. And though not all the entries led me to some greater understanding, I believed I was working toward something better. Even without getting to the absolute root of my discomfort, I knew that simply the act of writing—and many times, rereading—the stories I consistently told myself about who I am as a person shed light on how I handle stress and emotion. Oftentimes, as I grudgingly wrote when I'd rather have been eating the contents of my nearest 7-Eleven, I realized patterns in my pain.

In therapy, I worked on what I'd come to know as my deepest, saddest realization: I'd used food, in one extreme or another, as love and comfort and joy for twenty-some years. Amid the chaos of my childhood and the insecurity of my adulthood, I could control the food. When I felt nervous, food was reassuring. When I was anxious, food was soothing. When I was sad, food lifted me up. For every single emotion, I could turn to food.

What I hadn't realized until that point was that losing the weight meant turning away from food. It meant betraying my best friend. But I learned that as much as food comforted me, it hurt me, too. I had effectively stripped away the pounds that had protected me for so long, and now I was forced to stand naked in the world. Food had also been the bond in many of my relationships. I looked foreign to those I loved when I coldly turned away from our shared pastime. And even when Dad died seven years earlier, though my heart did shatter then, the food was there to help dull the feelings. Now, facing a different kind of sadness, I couldn't turn to eating to distract me.

Therapy helped me see my problems and understand them, but it didn't bring relief to my pain. The further down I dug to uncover the roots of my relationship with food and overeating, the worse I began to feel. It was like taking every belonging I owned out of the cabinets and closets and drawers of my house and having to stare at the mess of it without ever being able to put it all away. There was no closure to the chaos. When I relayed this to my therapist, she suggested I see a psychiatrist—someone who could evaluate me and potentially prescribe medication—in addition to our weekly meetings. I took the earliest available appointment.

After I sat down in the cold leather chair of the doctor's tiny office, she asked me, "So, let's talk about how you've been feeling lately. Not so good?"

I waited to construct my thoughts into something more coherent than crying.

"It's not that I want to die," I began. I paused, trying to find the words. "It's just that I want to go to sleep for a while."

"And why is that?" She tilted her head in caring concern.

"I don't know how much longer I can do all this." I looked around the room and out the window as if to wave at everything surrounding us to mean *all this*. "I guess it's just . . . life. It feels . . . so hard. Unbearable and . . . I don't know how to get through it. I don't know what to do with myself from minute to minute, how to fill the hours." Something about our conversation already made me embarrassed. I was ashamed that I couldn't just feel better. I wished contentment were like misplaced keys, something to search for and find.

She sat up straighter in her chair and then leaned forward. "Have you always felt this way?"

I looked down at my hands, considering. The sadness, the intense anxiety—they did feel oddly familiar. That writhing discomfort I so often experienced almost seemed as if it were part of me, something deeply innate. Pangs of nostalgic sadness hit me, one by one, memory by memory.

We talked a while longer, and I slowly came to consider the possibility that I'd always held this darkness somewhere inside of me.

Maybe my inner self weighed as heavily on me as my outer one once did.

She explained to me in fancier, more articulate terms that it seemed to her that I'd always suffered from depression—that it was likely something that ran in my family. Perhaps it was why Dad drank, she proposed. To soothe himself. To self-medicate. Perhaps it was why I ate. To soothe myself. To self-medicate.

And I knew she was right.

I hadn't known myself to be sad before I lost those 135 pounds. But now, without that numbing agent—the one that came in a two-pack with cream filling—I was alone with myself. I was exposed. I was left with emotions I'd eaten for twenty years.

She prescribed me an antidepressant, telling me that, no, it would not be a cure-all. The medication wouldn't make me happier or fix any of my problems, but it would help to lift the heavy cloud that was weighing me down and making me feel hopeless. She wanted me to be able to see beyond the gray fog I was stuck in, at least temporarily.

"Taking a medication to adjust this imbalance is not taking the easy way out. You're not taking drugs to feel amazing; you're taking them to feel normal." Her words calmed me. "The talk therapy is where you're working through it all."

Am I, though? I wondered. *Am I ever really going to get through it all?* I was sober from the food. I was a thin person reconciling with two decades of compulsive eating. It felt as if I'd drunk myself into oblivion at night, gotten sober by morning, and had to now clean up the house party I didn't realize I had thrown.

I stayed in therapy for the remainder of my senior year. And in the end, though I never felt as though the heavy fog lifted entirely,

I knew that I'd progressed. I realized that focusing on the control I could maintain with my body helped, at least subconsciously, to diminish my ability to feel unsettling emotions. In the past I avoided my feelings by consuming huge quantities of food. Now I avoided them by focusing on counting every calorie and carefully planning every meal. Food had always distracted me. Obsession left no room for anything else.

A part of getting to a healthier place was taking risks with food. With the guidance of my nutritionist, I learned—at times painfully slowly—to trust myself. That trust came from realizing that in order for me to heal my relationship with eating, food had to be a friend, not an enemy.

When I first admitted to myself that I had been dependent on food for the majority of my life, I was angry. I wanted to get as far away from it as possible, not to allow it to be my focus any longer. But something I'd heard another formerly morbidly obese man describe in a documentary about obesity stuck with me: "Food addiction isn't like addiction to alcohol or drugs, where you can just remove it from your life. With food, you need it to live. You have to have it every day." It was true. The only way to get through food addiction is by making peace with the food and uncovering the reasons we use food for anything other than hunger. I began to recognize the danger in attaching too much judgment to the foods I chose. Chocolate cake wasn't "bad," carrots weren't "good," and Bavarian cream doughnuts alone didn't make me morbidly obese. I was the one who abused the food and gave it character. I was the one who combined them all in massive quantities, eating well beyond fullness. I learned to view food as a neutral entity, not positive or negative.

By shifting the emphasis from my emotional bondage with food to a focus on building a new and healthy relationship with it, I was seizing a unique opportunity to start over. I regained an understanding that eating, while pleasurable, was not the be-all and end-all of my happiness.

Slowly, I could go out to eat with Daniel without an anxiety attack. Slowly, I could enjoy a social life like the one I once had, in which the extra calories from cocktails didn't unnerve me. I even took a spring break vacation with Nicole, Sabrina, Daniel, and his friends to Las Vegas—a trip that would have sent me into a panic just months earlier—and I reveled in the spontaneity of dining out.

The one area that still needed work was the range of foods I felt comfortable eating. I had begun to feel limited by the "safe" foods I'd clung to since losing weight. To branch out, my nutritionist encouraged me to bring back a few of the favorite foods I used to enjoy before losing weight. She suggested I try having one of these nostalgic treats in place of my afternoon snack. I thought long and hard about what those treats might be. Cupcakes, chocolate, doughnuts . . . just thinking about them was tumultuous. She instructed me to pick one, plate it, sit at a table, and eat it as slowly as I could, so that all my senses were engaged. For my first treat, I chose a cupcake. I followed her instructions: I set it on a pretty antique plate, brewed a steaming cup of tea, and ate it seated at the kitchen table for the better part of ten minutes. It was delightful. I'd made it special; I'd enjoyed it, and because of that—the eating lacked regret. And though I did wish I could have another, I didn't feel my old urge to binge. Day after day, I repeated my afternoon tea and cupcake. And after I had tried all the delicious flavors of cake and frosting, I moved on to chocolate bars. Dark, milk, white—it was sweet paradise. In time, I switched to doughnuts. The point of this daily dessert was proving to myself that I wasn't a monster around food. I would not eat with abandon anymore. I could have the foods that I loved and not abuse them, and I didn't have to live a life without them. And after a while of this healthy reintroduction to decadent food, I felt safer about how I used it to nourish me. I respected it, and in turn, I respected myself.

9

FOR SOMEONE STILL TRYING DEARLY TO MAKE PEACE with a new body, righting her mind to fit it, I could barely handle the thought of another transition. Leaving college upon graduation was the last thing I felt prepared to handle.

Take me back to Amherst was the only thought running through my mind as I moved the last of what seemed like thousands of boxes home to Medfield. I instantly missed the familiarity. I craved the routine, the normalcy of knowing what I had to do and when. For the first time, there was no planned next step. I had shuffled along through grade school—from ninth to tenth to eleventh and twelfth—and then I entered college. I was able to postpone living my own chosen path in life until at least twenty-two, when I graduated. And until that sunny May day, I made mostly dreamy plans about my future, mostly with Sabrina, and mostly while driving around in a car. I talked a talk as gigantic, as outlandish as I liked, because really, I didn't have to walk it yet. It felt comfortable for me—and, from what I gather, the entirety of my generation—to idealize the future and think everything would fall into place once I was done cycling through the education machine. Limitless possibilities, the ability to pursue anything, go anywhere, anytime. But the openness, the endless options paralyzed me. I thought of how much my family had sacrificed—everything Mom never had—just so that my future could be brighter. There was pressure with that large a gift. I began to feel the same way about life that I did about food. It was all a massive grocery store, and I had to choose the meal I most wanted to eat. *What if I chose the wrong one?*

I had no idea how I was going to find a job. The ones I applied for—through Craigslist and all kinds of print and online listings—rarely replied. Carefully crafted cover letters, résumés tailored to each position, each company—none of it seemed to matter. I never heard a word in reply, which only made the pursuit more agonizing. I wished I'd majored in something with an actual trade, like nursing or education. The undefined, broad nature of a communications degree wasn't doing me any favors in a hellish job market. "Broadcast journalism is a dying field," people would tell me. "People are going online to get their news, Andrea." In truth, I was, too. And perhaps I should have known that applying to the local affiliates for ABC, NBC, CBS, and Fox came with a certain level of difficulty. *But they've got to be looking for an intern,* I thought. *I'd be good at this.*

With no income, no apartment of my own, and tens of thousands of dollars of college loans to repay, I recognized that the sadness I'd worked through the year before had begun to reappear. I became more preoccupied with my eating. I noticed myself counting and recounting calories with greater precision, even adding to my total the sugar-free gum I chewed.

I picked fights with Daniel during our phone calls. Our dinner dates, when I'd drive out to visit him in Worcester, ended more often than not with both of us spewing hurtful words and my driving away. In every argument, I had a niggling sense that he had something over me—a sense that, since he'd seen me at my lowest, I should be grateful he'd stayed with me when anyone else might have walked away. He never said that outright, but still I resented my role as the one who struggled to feel good, the one who needed more emotionally. I also couldn't help but feel triggered by his extreme all-or-nothing eating—a behavior that caused him to regain all seventy-five pounds he'd lost the year before. If Daniel wasn't dieting and eating cleanly, he was bingeing; there was no middle ground. As someone recovering from both extreme modes of eating, it was difficult to watch.

Slowly I pulled away, unable to feel even a tickle of the romance we once had. Daniel was no longer my boyfriend. Instead, he was a parent, a caretaker. And even outside of the two of us, I couldn't reconcile, couldn't accept, that life after college wasn't going as I'd hoped and expected. I wanted everything to be different, to be better, to be new. So I left him. I broke his heart and mine by ending our relationship.

I thought I could start over. I thought that he had encumbered me and that leaving him would feel like stretching my legs after sitting cramped in a too-small airplane seat. I thought that I hadn't experienced enough of love to be so devout, so committed to one person.

It turned out that none of those thoughts proved entirely true. A greater despair sprouted within me, and I realized I missed Daniel. I missed familiarity and security and ease. I missed the team we were. Several times a day I wanted to call him, if only to hear him call me "Andie" like he used to. The days—the ones that already left me bored and restless after graduation—grew longer, duller.

I took a job waitressing at an Outback Steakhouse when I could no longer cope with the constant rejection I experienced everywhere else. For half a year, I put on a mustard-yellow shirt that sat like a box on my still-foreign body, affixed various pins for the required amount of "flair," and made three dollars an hour plus tips. I pretended I was on an episode of *Punk'd* anytime a customer gave me grief. *This has to be a prank,* I said to myself, smiling.

Passing the months without Daniel slowly became easier, more normal. I hung out with friends I hadn't seen in a while. I busied myself with hobbies and activities I hadn't pursued while we were together—crafty things like scrapbooking and greeting-card making. I went to the movies, alone. The hardest part wasn't finding new activities; it was filling the emotional void that existed without him. Daniel had been my best friend, confidant, therapist, and adviser, and now that he was gone, I felt as if I had none of those things. I was stripped. I couldn't be weak, even if I felt it. I couldn't be needy, even if I wanted to be. Having to face the world without him, I was forced to muster more strength from within. And in time, I did.

In February, a film crew took up residence in Medfield. A real, live Hollywood film crew—helmed by none other than Martin Scorsese—chose my sleepy little town to film a movie.

I'd heard, weeks before, that they'd picked the Medfield State Hospital, a sprawling mental institution that had been shut down for nearly a decade, as the set for *Shutter Island,* a film based on the thriller book by Dennis Lehane, author of other novels-turned-movies, including *Mystic River* and *Gone, Baby, Gone.* The building sat eerily up on Hospital Hill, removed from town and just aged enough to feel cold and creepy. It was the kind of place you were sure held disturbing secrets and an interesting history, somewhere you'd never want to find yourself alone in the dark. Mostly we townspeople used the land around it for soccer games and sledding, and, as such, we weren't displaced. We were hardly jostled.

I was ecstatic. Having loved movies my whole life through, and having studied film in Amherst and Rome, this was just too good to be true. Not only was it Martin Scorsese, my favorite director, but it was Leonardo DiCaprio, my favorite human being, as well. Fate seemed at play.

Weeks earlier, I'd gone to a casting call to be an extra on the film but was never contacted. A few of the film's production offices—the art and construction departments—were set up directly across the street from my house in an unused office building. One afternoon I mustered enough courage to walk over and try to give someone my résumé and the brief cover letter I'd written, one unlike any I'd penned in the hopes of landing a job. I'd become disheartened by the pretension of the traditional cover letter. The navel gazing, the polite sucking-up—neither had worked in the months before when I wrote and rewrote to what seemed like every available job in New England. Knowing that I really had no qualifications for this position, I got creative. I explained that while I didn't have any previous experience working in film, I knew the area around the set well and could be useful in many ways as a local. You need to know where to buy something? I'm your girl. You need delicious lunch spots? I'm your girl. You need directions? I'm your girl. *Or I will google it and pretend to have known it all along.*

I expressed my love of film, the fact that I'd studied it in college and abroad, but I really just aimed to let whoever would read the letter know how much I wanted to help in any way. I highlighted what I could truly offer to do for them: any old thing. The whole letter read as, "Hey, I'm really good at shoveling if we get a snow-storm!"

I handed my nearly pathetic résumé and that letter to a nice woman, who said she'd pass it on to the art department coordinator. Three weeks passed without a word, and I had started to come to terms with the fact that this film wasn't in the cards for me.

Then I got a phone call. I was mid-drive home from running errands on a Monday, already dreading my shift at Outback that evening, when the art department coordinator rang me. She said that one of her assistants had to have emergency surgery, so they were looking for someone to fill in until Friday. Could I come in for a quick interview? I raced home, tore through my clothes to find the perfect thing to wear, and sped over to the office.

"Lori Lopes," she introduced herself, outstretching her hand. With a head of thick, shiny raven hair, she was a beautiful doppel-gänger for Mary-Louise Parker. She smiled sweetly.

I like her. I could tell instantly.

For thirty minutes she walked me around the office, giving me the lay of the land and a clear picture of what they did in the art department. Essentially, she told me, I would be working as a pro-duction assistant and perhaps also helping out in the set decorating department, if need be. The art department was run in tandem by the production designer, Academy Award–winner Dante Ferretti, and the art director, four-time Academy Award–nominee Bob Guerra. The set decorating was handled exclusively by Academy Award winner Francesca Lo Schiavo, who also happened to be

Dante's wife. These three worked with brilliant teams of artists and decorators to draft large-scale drawings of what they envisioned each scene of the film to look like—all in line with Dante's overall artistic vision. They designed everything, creating every nook and cranny, every slight detail of the spaces that would later be built by the construction department.

I was terrified. I spent that Tuesday to the following Friday barely sleeping, working as hard and passionately as I ever had. To call it thrilling would be a crazed understatement. I was high for four days straight on paint fumes and Leonardo DiCaprio sightings. Hour by hour, the job changed. I drove from set to set, dropping off the set designs at various departments, running errands, anything that needed doing. I was eager; I was hungry for more.

Lori took notice. At certain moments in the day, as I was running to and fro around the office, smiling like a self-important fool excited just to be making coffee for a feature film crew, I'd catch her looking at me and smiling to say, *Thank you.* The whole department knew how much I loved what I was doing. And in turn, they liked me for it. New to their world, I was one of the few yet to be jaded by the harshness of the entertainment business. I was green and still idealistic about showbiz. Like a kid who still believes in Santa, they wanted to preserve my excitement. Each day, I arrived at the office a full hour before anyone else in the morning and stayed late to close it all down at night. I brought in coffee cake from my favorite bakery, Mom's famous homemade lemon squares, and chocolate éclairs from the finest French pastry shop in Boston. Twelve-hour shifts flew by before I knew it, because I never sat down. The excitement, the nonstop nature of the business kept me so energetic, I buzzed. It wasn't simply that I was starstruck; I was working on something I cared about deeply.

By three p.m. on Friday, I caught wind that Jo, who I'd been filling in for, would indeed be back come Monday. My heart sank, thinking that it was all about to be over. I pondered my return to Outback as I ran to the nearest bakery to buy John Michael, my handsome new friend and fellow art department assistant, a birthday cake, complete with candles and a card. Lori and I had hoped to surprise him before we all left for the weekend. She and I had gotten so close so quickly. I reveled in the last few hours that day. When John Michael had blown out the candles, Lori pulled me aside for a moment while the others stood around clapping.

When we'd walked a few feet away from the group, she hugged me. She pulled back to look me in the eyes and said, "Andrea, look. I just want to let you know that this week has been overwhelmingly wonderful with you here. I can't tell you how much I've loved it. And, while you were gone this afternoon, we all talked here, and"—she gestured toward all those standing in the room—"we want you to stay for the whole run of the film."

I was floored. There was nothing I wanted to hear more than "stay."

Suddenly, the room was quiet. I turned to face the department and found them all standing there, smiling my way. A round of clapping to show their support, a boisterous set of cheers to congratulate me. When the applause softened, I made sure to thank each of them.

"This has been such a pleasure. I'm so very happy to stay," I told the group, grinning.

When does this happen to people? To me? I wondered. I turned my head skyward, not sure if I should thank whoever, whatever was up there blessing me.

"And, well, just so everyone knows . . . ," I began. The room quieted. "If Leo and I should run away together because he's finally come to his senses and decided he's just not that into leggy blonde supermodels anymore, I just want you all to know . . . well, I just wouldn't feel right leaving without telling you all . . . it's been real."

They laughed. I held my face straight and serious, half of me joking while the other half of me mused, *Hey, it could happen.*

The weeks that followed flew by at an alarming speed. Each day was a heady mix of frenzy and fun. I made fast friends with nearly everyone who worked on- and off-set. Aside from traditional production assistant duties, I also jumped at two opportunities to temporarily assist Dante and Francesca, separately. Much of it involved my driving a minivan around tight Boston streets and liaising between production departments. But it also meant time spent very close to the director's chair. It allowed me to watch scenes between Ben Kingsley and Mark Ruffalo, and my beloved Leonardo DiCaprio, and to jump at Marty Scorsese's voice as he shouted, "Cut!" and "Action!" I worked hard to project an air of confidence, some semblance of a casual *Ahem, I'm supposed to be here.* Mostly I stared, transfixed at Leo. He seemed kind, playful, certainly as wonderfully skilled an actor as I'd always known him to be. Beyond his good looks, I respected his work, his choices. *This Boy's Life, What's Eating Gilbert Grape, The Aviator, The Departed*—his filmography ran like credits through my mind. I didn't only want to grab his face and kiss him, I wanted to tell him how deeply I admired him as an actor and artist. But, really, the kiss would have sufficed.

Eleven years earlier, in December 1997—just a month after we'd been told that Dad had died—*Titanic* hit theaters. That whole year prior, when Dad had gone missing, Mom and I busied ourselves as best we could. We bided our time with movies and eating. Romantic comedies, dramas, thrillers, period pieces—it hardly mattered what we saw, only that we left our present minds for a few hours. We went to the theater nearly four times a week. When he died, it felt as if someone had pressed Pause on life. And yet, somehow, it resumed. Mom returned to work and I to school. The first month was a blur. Mom and I went to see Titanic a week after it hit theaters, knowing we'd like it. We'd always admired Leo, and Kate Winslet, well, she was perfection in our minds—a compelling actress, a porcelain doll with that unforgettable face. The two of them sharing the screen together was naturally wonderful. Plus, we'd heard all the buzz about the crazed swarms of moviegoers, the box office record breaking.

For the three hours of runtime, we sat in rapture. Leaving the theater and driving home, we barely talked. Already, I was fiending to rewatch it. The next day, we returned to the theater. And again the day after. For weeks on end, Mom and I went to see *Titanic* over and over. School nights at ten p.m., weekends twice in a row, whenever there was a showing. And the times when we were told that the movie was sold out, as it so often was, Mom got this look in her eyes. A desperate, wounded look. Her lips would part, and she'd stare at the box office attendant as if to plead, *Please, I need this.* Seeing the devastation in her eyes, without fail, they'd find her two open seats somewhere in the packed theater.

In all, I went to see *Titanic* twenty times, and Mom, twenty-two. Each time felt like the first. When it left theaters, Mom and I felt an odd sense of loss. I knew others who had seen it as many times, some more. There was a mania surrounding that movie. But us? I always wondered why we'd become so obsessed. Mom was a grown woman, after all, and a world-weary one at that. She wasn't the kind to fawn over a movie so severely. Everyone thought we were unhinged, crazy. "The ship sinks, for Christ's sake! Like, okay, we get it." I couldn't, she couldn't, articulate what brought us back to see it, time after time. *Why did we go all those tens of times when we barely had money to buy groceries?*

Years later, Mom and I talked about our *Titanic* days. We smiled, sort of laughing at ourselves for being such intense fans. "Gosh, we were insane, weren't we?" we commiserated. I looked at her, shaking her head at the memory.

"I really loved that, Mom."

"Me, too. And, y'know, I get it now. The movie—it just let me cry."

She looked out the window, taken by the thought. She went on, "When Dad died and we went to the theater, I think it was the only time I felt like I could sit in the dark and cry. For three hours, anyway."

I fell silent, searching her face for more. *God, I love this woman.* I smiled at her through tears.

"Me, too, Mumma. Me, too."

When I introduced myself to Leo at his champagne and oyster party, that conversation came rushing back. I thought of Mom. *She'd love to be here.*

That week, I had been tasked with assisting Francesca. Just looking at her gave a hint at her importance. Graceful, the epitome of class, she was petite and well put together—a blond beauty. Every day, she strolled into the office with clothes so crisp and well styled, you'd swear she had just plucked them from the window display at

Ralph Lauren. She and I got along famously. Known for being a bit particular, a bit fussy-meets-handful, she was softer, gentler with me. Our rapport was sweet in a way it wasn't between her and the others, those who thought her to be a diva.

During our drives to the set from her posh Boston loft, she'd recline in the backseat of the van and offer me life advice in her syrupy thick Italian accent. "Do one theeng, Andrea," she purred. "Peeeck one theeng and do eet well. Geeve eet eva-ry-theeng you are, eva-ry-theeng you have." I sensed that she wanted the best for me in the same manner she might want for her daughter. Francesca loved her work, and was loved for her work. The night of Leo's champagne party, she invited me into her apartment for wine. She scoffed at any notion of arriving on time. "We relaax here. Then, we go," she informed me. *Fashionably late works for her.* I nodded at the thought.

There, in the wealthy expanse of apartment in Boston's most affluent section, she sat with me on her couch, and we spent nearly an hour in what she coolly called "girrrl talk," her voice rolling over the *r*'s like tires on gravel. I nearly died when she pointed to her side table, the one that held her Oscar. "Hold eet, peek eet up!" I did, marveling at its weight.

The moment we arrived at the event, I wished I'd had time to run home and change clothes By nine p.m., after working all day, my hair was wild in curls from the humidity, my black scoop-neck tee and white Bermuda shorts both seeming dowdy, given the swankiness of the outdoor party. Tables surrounded us, covered in starched white linen. Raw oysters sat neatly in rows on wide beds of ice. Dozens of champagne flutes stood on silver platters, glowing bright like candles in the dark.

As I silently cursed myself for looking a mess, I caught sight of him. Backwards baseball cap, white tee, with a hoodie tied loose and low around his hips, he leaned his head back in a laugh with a group of producers. *Leo, Leo, Leo.* In an outfit as casual as mine, he looked like a Calvin Klein ad.

Across the room, I noticed Mark Ruffalo talking to a circle of my friends, the PAs. The man was a ten-foot radius of charisma. All who stood near him seemed content and at ease. I felt a pull toward him, wanting to be closer to someone who exuded such positive energy. His face was kind, youthful from the innocence of his smile. His hair was a mess of black curls, not unlike my own.

I grabbed two champagne flutes from the table beside me and passed one to Francesca. "I go talk to Marteee." She nodded toward Martin Scorsese, sitting with his wife at the table in the far corner. I brought the champagne to my mouth and watched her walk toward them, pure confidence in every last stride of her slim legs. *I think I'm dehydrated,* I thought to myself, glancing down at the nearly empty flute. *He sprang for the good stuff, I bet.*

The bubbles made me bold. I walked over to the PA circle surrounding Mark Ruffalo. Chatting with a friend, I couldn't help but make eye contact with Mark. He smiled. I finished the sentence I'd begun, excused myself, and made my way three feet over to stand in front of Mark. I outstretched my hand to him, grinning. "I've been wanting to meet you!" On the last of these uncool words, I felt like crawling below the table to my left. Without skipping a beat, he returned a laugh and an enthusiastic hello. The genuine nature of his smile let me know that he wasn't, in fact, mocking me. His sincerity disarmed me. I was wooed into a kind of comfort I never, ever expected to feel with a movie star. In seconds, our conversation struck up like a match sliding quickly across the rough edge of its box. It was effortless—natural, even. For ten minutes we went back and forth, talking about life in New York versus LA, culture, film, what I should do with my career—the advice alone was valuable.

When we were finally interrupted, as someone pulled him away for a word, I smiled genuinely at him. He returned the same smile with, "Well, listen, it's been great talking to you. See you tomorrow?"

And I may have been a touch overeager in saying yes. I surveyed the party once more and noticed Leo standing alone now. *Should I? Shouldn't I?*

Oh, what the hell.

I set my empty champagne flute down and moved confidently toward him. Steps away, I realized the gravity of what was about to happen and wanted suddenly, desperately, to turn back. *I cannot waltz up to Leonardo DiCaprio out of nowhere. I cannot.* As I was about to turn on my heel, ready to call the whole plan off, our eyes met.

I wished for the power of invisibility, but when that proved a nonoption, I relented. *Just go.* I walked the remaining feet to meet him.

"Uh, hi! Hello! I'm, uh—I'm Andrea."

His mouth widened in a closed-mouth grin. "Leo," he spoke, nodding as if to say, *How do you do?*

Marry me.

"It's nice to meet you." I smiled sheepishly.

"You, too," he said, still grinning politely.

"This is a great party you've thrown. Thanks for having us." I stuttered no fewer than seven times per sentence.

"Yeah, it's fun." He surveyed the scene, obviously happy to see everyone enjoying themselves. "I'm just hoping that all the raw oysters I had shipped in—I'm just hoping everyone eats them all." He let out a small laugh.

I laughed, nodding. "Yeah, well, hey! I'll do my best to eat the remainder."

As we exchanged mundane pleasantries, my excited and champagne-addled brain made me think, *Are we flirting?* My insides clenched.

"Oh, and, um, do you think we could get a picture together?" And with that, I'd done it. Put myself out there. I'd become the fan.

He assessed my face, his look one part shy, one part flattered. "Sure."

I scanned the people around us, looking for some unsuspecting individual to snap a picture with my phone. "Jeremy, can you take a picture of us?"

He took the phone from my hand and moved a good five feet away from us as we posed. Leo's hand slid behind my back, wrapping securely around my waist and resting on my hip. Every muscle in my core tightened. I silently screamed before my breathing ceased. I moved my arm around his back, my hand landing high on his shoulder blade, and I leaned into him. If I could have frozen the moment in time, just stayed right there forever, I'd have done it without hesitation.

We smiled. I heard the faux-snap sound of my phone's camera, and I tensed, knowing the moment was over. He released my hip and moved his hand across my back, stepping away. Before we could fully part, I heard, "Ooh, wait a sec! Let me snap a photo of you two!" I turned and saw the script supervisor, Martha. I grinned.

We reconnected, positioning ourselves the same way as before. I couldn't contain a huge, toothy smile. Martha held up her camera, then lowered it slightly to look at us over the lens. "This'll be on all the entertainment shows tomorrow—just wait. 'Hollywood's new beautiful couple.'"

I died.

Can we make this happen?! I begged internally. Part of me felt nervous that Leo would be uncomfortable with such a suggestion. *Us? A couple? Who?* Before I got to the end of my thought, he laughingly sang, "Duh na na na na na!"

I died again.

Still unbreathing, I asked myself, *Did Leo just sing the* Entertainment Tonight *jingle?*

Martha offered a laugh. "I can call these things." She raised the camera again and snapped the photo.

I couldn't die again, but if I could have, I would have.

I had a hot flash. Three of them, unrelenting and burning, in a row. We pulled apart and smiled at each other. I'd just opened my mouth to continue our conversation, when I heard her Italian tongue trilling around my name. "Andrrrrrrrea!"

I turned to see Francesca, now standing beside us. "Andrea, there you are! Come. We go." She smiled sweetly, nodding to the car. Her hand rose to caress Leo's face.

He smiled at her. They'd worked on movies together before. Marty, Dante, Francesca, Bob Guerra—they worked as a team as often as they could manage.

"We are tired. We go. Good night!" She tilted her head to the side as she gazed fondly at Leo.

He let out a sigh. "Good night, ladies," he said quietly. Francesca had already begun walking toward the parking lot.

I gave in and smiled. "Have a good night." I turned and followed her, hating every last step.

I barely remembered dropping Francesca at her apartment;

my body and mind were still zinging in euphoria. I pulled my cell phone from my pocket and looked at the clock, noting that it was one a.m. I called her anyway.

"Andrea?" She sounded half asleep, her breathing like a gentle snore.

"Mumma, I talked to him."

Her breath hitched. Instantly she perked up. She squealed. "Leo! Imagine that."

"Yeah." My lips spread so far in either direction, I wasn't sure they'd stay contained on my face. I loved her for knowing how much it meant to me.

To her.

To us.

10

FROM THE WAY I APPEARED, people might have assumed I was doing exceptionally well. I worked twelve-hour days five and sometimes six days per week on the movie set without complaint; I multitasked with dazzling proficiency; I was perky, upbeat, and presentable at all times, with hair and makeup perfectly done. The only person who could have known how truly exhausted I felt was me. And I could only blame myself for feeling so ragged. Although I'd worked hard to mend my disordered eating, now I had to face another truth: I was addicted to exercise.

One year earlier, at the end of senior year of college, after reaching my goal weight, I developed sciatica—a pinched nerve—on my left side. Moving my left leg in any direction, I felt a stabbing and burning sensation in my left buttock. It developed because I'd never properly rested once I started a strict workout routine. I'd run four miles, seven days a week, without ever letting myself take a day off. I felt tethered to the treadmill, terrified of gaining any weight back. I had no frame of reference for the amount of rest a person needed when she'd just lost half of her starting body weight. The food—well, I was working on it. But the running, each of the miles I cursed jogging daily—I wasn't so sure I could stop. It seemed such a crucial part of my success in losing weight. I'd always heard that of all the solo exercises one could do, running is the biggest calorie torcher. I was convinced that no other method of movement would provide such a burn. But the strain, the overuse of my poor, tired legs, triggered the sciatica, and I was forced to stop running for a month. One terrifying month. I struggled through sessions on the elliptical and the arc trainer; I tried to walk; I could barely sleep without aching nerve pain in my left side. I was an anxious wreck, thinking I would pack on any pounds lost.

When my body healed from the nerve pain, I returned to running. I kept it up for a full year, still motivated by the fear that quitting meant gaining weight.

I hated running. It was no longer fun. I no longer felt accomplished or rejuvenated or energized after I stepped off the treadmill. By then, I'd even begun to resent *The View*, my favorite TV program to pound out the miles to. I was drained. I thought for sure that the only way I would be thin, stay thin, was by keeping on keeping on. I started to fear my future. *How could I keep this up? How do I continue running so many miles, so consistently, each and every day, when I hate it so?* Running felt compulsive, dreadful, punishing, like an abusive relationship. I'd fall asleep at night dreading, dreading, dreading the next morning, when I'd have to run again.

Now, coupled with the growing hours on set, the running felt even more brutal. My body, my mind—both were exhausted. I sat in my car one night, after a particularly long day, and I let my head fall to hit the steering wheel. The parking lot was empty. I was supposed to be heading to the gym; I hadn't run yet that day.

"I can't," I whispered, with no one to talk to but the odometer.

My shoulders began to bounce up and down in the makings of a sob. The rumbling felt deep and guttural, a cry I wouldn't be able to tame. Soon the tears came.

"I can't," I repeated.

I pulled the keys from the ignition.

"I can't. I can't." I said it over and over until I actually believed it.

While talking myself into and out of the run, I suddenly had a startling thought: *I'd almost rather be fat.*

Surely I wouldn't rather that. I didn't prefer discomfort, a body less capable of moving me, and the way the world looked down at me when I was big. But perhaps I preferred the ease. The way I was punishing myself now, was it all worthwhile? Does looking good cost feeling good?

Am I even happy?

I did not lose 135 pounds only to find myself in an unhappy marriage to running. And if I did, I wanted a divorce.

I did not lose 135 pounds because my sanity mattered less than vanity.

I decided in that moment that I would try my best to let myself find the weight I was supposed to be. If not running every day, or not running ever again, meant that I would gain 5 pounds, then I would accept each one of them. If 10 pounds were in store for me, then so be it. Truly, I would let myself be.

I would live the way I wanted to live, without feeling a tremendous sense of dread each morning when I opened my eyes and knew the treadmill was there, without feeling as if my being at a healthy weight for the first time in my whole life hinged on desperate exercise.

Those first three minutes after I'd made my decision felt intensely free. Because when I had made my mind up that I would lose the weight forever, I had also made my mind up that I would be happy first.

I thought that in losing, I was finally cutting ties with what I perceived to be a fatal, lifelong hindrance. My personal handicap. I wanted to be free of worrying about my size. I wanted to forget that I was uncomfortable in front of people and just let myself be, without feeling painfully aware of how big I was. In trying to find this freedom, I created another prison. I ran from weight, and then I ran from weight some more. I felt shackled by exercise just as I'd felt shackled by my weight. And when I realized what I'd done— when depression settled in as my default state—I said, *I'd rather be what I was than what I am now.*

And that shocked my eyes open.

When I felt the tears had been wrung out of my eyes like a thoroughly squeezed sponge, I started the car, reversed, and drove home.

The following day after work, I pondered what my future with exercise would be. Running or not, I wouldn't give up on moving; I understood the importance of exercise as part of a healthy life. What I wanted was to find an activity that was gentler on my body and less daunting to my mind.

At the gym where I had a yearlong membership, I considered the elliptical machine, knowing that the smooth, gliding motion would be easy on my joints. The problem was that the few times I'd used it in the past, my toes had gone numb for some odd reason. I decided to try the StairMaster, since all four of the machines were unoccupied. It took a brief four minutes for me to hop off winded, red faced, cursing, and never to return again. *So that's why all the stair climbers had been available,* I thought to myself, panting. I turned to see the familiar treadmill, and a long walk crossed my mind. At the magazine rack, I grabbed the most recent issue of *O* and hopped onto an available machine. The belt slid backward, jostling me as I set the machine to four miles per hour and the incline at a moderate 2 percent. The fifteen-minute-mile pace was comfortable, considering it was the speed at which I'd warmed up my legs for all my runs. With the magazine placed over the display panel, it covered all mentions of time, calories burned, and distance. I didn't want to concern myself with the numbers; I only wanted to gauge how much I liked what I was doing. With earbuds in place, I pressed Play on my iPod. I walked until I finished reading, cover to cover, and only then did I lift the magazine to see how far I'd traveled. Fifty minutes. Three and a quarter miles. I blinked a few times at the screen, incredulous. For two years, I'd run nearly that same mileage on the treadmill and hated every second of it, but now, while walking and reading, I'd enjoyed it. I was shocked at how easy it had felt, how quickly the time had passed without my agonizing over the clock. Content, I stepped off the machine to leave. I hadn't even reached the end of the row of treadmills when the worry set in. I stopped, tuning in to the obsessive part of me— the one that urged me to question the calories I'd just burned. *Maybe I should walk a bit more.* I had barely broken a sweat.

But no. *No.*

Before I could even think a moment longer, I stuffed the magazine back into its slot on the rack and left the gym, determined to not undermine the progress I'd made.

The next day after work, I returned to the gym and read while walking on the treadmill. Again, it was pleasurable. Again, I had to convince myself it was enough.

Slowly, over the course of two months, I stopped questioning its validity as a calorie burner and instead started recognizing that movement, in any form, was beneficial. I even came to look forward to the time I spent on long walks. It was restorative, meditative, and not at all punishing and dreadful like the days when my joints ached on impact. I could do it anywhere, at any time, with anyone. Heading to the gym after work wasn't a chore but a way to unwind. I had found a comfortable pace, podcasts to listen to that interested me, friends who wanted to walk with me on the weekends, beautiful trails by my house to explore, new magazines to subscribe to, and music that made me want to move.

Each week when I weighed myself, I prepared for a gain. With all of the peace I'd gained from walking, I could accept five pounds. It was worth that much. So when the scale never changed, week after week, I was surprised. Logically, I knew that the miles I covered—whether jogged or strolled—were roughly the same, but it took the proof of my stable weight for me to really believe it. The only explanation that seemed to make sense to me was that by lightening up on movement—no longer engaging in excessive cardio—I wasn't constantly ravenous, which meant that I didn't feel as if I were always fighting against hunger. With a less intense form of exercise, it was easier to eat three healthy meals a day and two snacks and feel satisfied. I also wasn't drained all the time, which gave me the energy to actually want to move my body. I recognized the positive cycle I'd begun: move moderately, eat moderately, repeat.

*　*　*

After *Shutter Island* wrapped, I spent the next six months living like a Generation Y cliché. My new contacts in the film industry didn't have any work immediately available, so I lived at home with Mom and Paul. Kate was also unemployed, so we spent our time aimlessly hanging out in the same way we did during summers home from college, trying to avoid the plunge into the real world. I halfheartedly looked for work in local television production once again.

During that period of professional limbo, I began to slowly reconcile my relationship with Daniel. I called him often. We met for dinners. I was awestruck by the life he'd made while we were apart. He had moved to Cambridge, where he made a living as a professional poker player. Hearing him describe it, I thought back to the day he began playing poker, during our first week of freshman year at UMass. He sat in a circle in the lounge, Justin to his right, a few of our friends occupying the seats to his left, chips and cards littered about the wooden table. They all began playing nonstop. It was the year that Texas Hold'em blew up. It was everywhere—on TV, on every floor of my dorm. Soon the live games moved online to sites like PokerStars, and one by one, our friends started making serious money. Daniel was always good at the game. And while I had been working on *Shutter Island*, he'd won a handful of tournaments that led him to play in major events all around the world.

I loved that he'd gained such independence and found success while pursuing an alternative career. It excited and inspired me. Spending time with him—watching movies, strolling the narrow streets of his Cambridge neighborhood, laughing the way we used to—was fulfilling. I was quickly reminded of that familiar, deeply contented feeling Daniel gave me.

"I love you," I blurted out, as we stood at the door to his

apartment after dinner one night in July. Nearly dropping his keys, he turned to face me, revealing eyes that were at once stunned and happy. He grabbed my waist with both hands and drew me in for a kiss.

"I love you, too," he said, his lips barely parting with mine.

"Daniel, I—I'm so sorry. For everything."

He tensed, pulling back slightly, and looked down, pausing a moment before nodding. "I know." Suddenly, he was more timid, and I knew that my apology had reminded him of when I'd shattered his heart. He entwined his fingers with mine. "I just missed you."

After a week of talking things through, we'd decided to get back together. Our reunion left me feeling restored. It was as if a part of me had been missing and was suddenly returned, and all I wanted to do was to ensure that I'd never lose it again.

At the start of August, Daniel traveled to Europe with his two best friends. The Saturday he left, I'd just returned from a long walk and was moments from stepping into a cool shower when I caught sight of my naked body in the bathroom mirror. I stopped and stared at my reflection. My frame was lithe, thin. Until my waist, the reflection I saw of me was one I liked. But as my eyes moved lower to my belly and beyond, I winced. Circling my belly was an inner tube of sagging flesh. Twenty years with an overbearing middle, a belly so protruding and bossy, my skin hadn't taken kindly to the dramatic loss. The fat that once filled the two cascading rolls was gone, and what stayed behind was a double sash of deflated skin. It had no more elasticity. Loose and wrinkled, the skin sagged in the way it would on the body of someone nearing ninety. I could pinch the hanging flaps and find my fingers almost touching between the thin sheets of skin.

My gaze moved farther downward in the mirror, and I saw the same sagging sacks between my legs. My inner thighs looked as deflated, as dimpled with wear and age, as my midsection. I shook my body and watched as the pounds of sagging skin flapped up, down, up, down. Each bounce of empty flesh weighed heavy on the downswing.

I cursed it. *Why has the fat left, but you—you won't go away?* It embarrassed me in a way my full belly never could have. This was the new body I'd worked so hard to have. This was the body I was working so hard to *love*. The skin that hung behind after I'd lost all the weight felt mocking, humiliating. I feared anyone ever touching it, couldn't bear the thought of them noticing it as they grabbed me in a hug. Even being naked in front of Daniel made me feel unnervingly vulnerable. "I know it's ugly!" I wanted to shout apologetically at him as I squeezed my eyes shut when we began kissing, so wishing the lights were out.

With clothes on, the skin masked itself well. Shirts hung loosely at my middle. Jeans with some measure of stretch could snugly hold the skin on my thighs taut. But when I moved, I felt the excess bounce. It would slap against my body in a punishing way.

You did this to yourself, you know. I chastised myself silently. Part of me felt I deserved it, but mostly I wondered of its finality. *Must I walk around with this, my cross to bear, for the rest of my life?* It felt odd to have worked so diligently to carve this body out of the mass it once was for it now to look so unattractive to me. Different, yes, but distressing all the same. Stretch marks swam up my front, my back, like silvery white fish. I was sympathetic toward the skin that bore them, having stretched so far beyond its limits that red veins emerged where it simply could not bear to stretch farther. The markings, now faded, I could live with. But the excess skin plagued me. During the first year the weight was off, I felt a nagging sense that I had more weight to lose whenever I'd see the sagging. It drove me mad that it never tightened, never rebounded, no matter how much I exercised. No amount of squats, lunges, crunches, or planks helped it to recoil. I learned, perhaps much too late to prevent the excessive exercise, that this excess that hung low on my belly and thighs was not the same as flab. There wasn't any fat left inside the pockets to blast away. I'd done all of that.

Mom saw how self-conscious I'd become about it. She'd pull my shoulders back when she caught me hunching, folding inwardly on myself to cover it. She watched as I stared into dressing room mirrors, unclothed and unhappy. We had talked about how deeply bothered I was by it.

And when she felt it weighing equally as heavy on my mind as it did on my body, we made an appointment with a plastic surgeon.

At the consultation, he proposed an abdominoplasty. Horrified at the graphic discussion, I looked away as he explained to Mom what would occur during the procedure. Essentially, he would slice a bowed line widthwise across my abdomen that would be curved in the same upturn as a smile. After releasing my belly button so the skin could effectively rise in a clean, single sheet above my abdomen, he would then pull that sheet downward. When the skin was pulled sufficiently taut to meet the bottom curved incision, he would cut off the remaining skin. He'd then take the skin from my upper abdomen and stitch it to lower portion of skin above my pubic bone. It made sense and disgusted me all at once. Squeamish,

I could barely listen as he discussed how he could rectify the hanging skin on each inner thigh.

Leaving the appointment that day, Mom and I spent the car ride in serious discussion. It was a lot to consider. The surgery would require me to be put under general anesthesia for nearly three hours. It would also mean one night's stay in the hospital. I'd be fairly immobile for the days following surgery, laid up with two small bottle drains inserted into my midsection to drain the fluids that naturally accumulate postsurgery. Tubes the size of drinking straws would connect the drains from outside my pelvis to inside my abdomen and be sewn in place on my skin. I'd have to empty these drains twice daily, noting the amount of fluid on a chart. They'd be removed after one week, and the holes left from the tubes would close and seal over time. In all, recovery would last about three weeks. And what was more, my insurance would not cover the cost of surgery, which neared $15,000 for the abdominoplasty and thigh-skin removal combined. Since the skin was not technically causing any rashes or some other serious health condition, it was deemed medically unnecessary—an elective surgery. Despite several appeal attempts and my surgeon's writing a letter to the insurance company to note that I was living with five pounds of excess skin hanging from my body, the company would not reconsider. It was difficult to hear the insurance rejection over and over. *If they deem it elective, is this all just superficial of me? Am I considering the equivalent of a face-lift?*

But the truth was that this was more than a beauty fix. After all the arduous work of losing weight, I was still deeply unhappy with my body. The only way I'd be able to be fully comfortable was if I got the excess skin removed. I couldn't find it in me to justify keeping it at twenty-three years old. I consulted Mom and Daniel, and both of them supported me. After careful consideration, weighing every pro and con of such a major surgery, I decided to go through with it. Mom withdrew the money from her retirement account to pay for it.

At the end of August, on a muggy Friday morning, I awoke in post-op to Mom's voice. "Baby, it's all over. You're out of surgery." The room spun. All I could feel was an unbearable heaviness, a weight compressing my whole body.

After one full day of recovery in the hospital, I was allowed to go home. The days that followed were painful. Turning to Mom on the second day at home, I told her, "This is worse than I imagined."

"Sweetie," she said gently, "just wait until you have kids."

I shuddered at the thought. It felt as if a boulder had been placed upon my stomach, and it was trapping me, making movement impossible, crushing me slowly. My breathing was shallow and labored. I was confined to lying horizontally in bed, with my only outings being trips to the bathroom. And those were quite challenging, since the numbness in my core made it nearly impossible to contract the muscles in my abdomen and pelvis. I could feel an extreme tightness, a pulling at the seams where my thighs had been sewn. The painkillers I'd been prescribed helped, but they made me nauseated. And when I'd throw up, my heaving would be so violent that I'd fear my stitches had ripped open. Looking at the drains that were stitched into my skin also made me queasy; they held a disgusting, phlegm-like fluid that emptied out from within me. Twice daily, Mom or Paul had to remove them for cleaning—a gross chore that I felt bad about asking them to do.

After the first few days, the weeks of recovery moved by quickly.

I wore a tight brace around my middle for a full month. It took even longer before I felt comfortable touching my midsection, before I felt any sensation in the area at all. Touching my belly felt faint and distant, as though a barrier stood between the skin my fingers touched outside and the now-hardened inside.

It was still hard to look in the mirror, but for a different reason. I had a deep red scar in the shape of a smile on my belly. My thighs showed a slicing red line where my legs met my pelvis. Somehow, though, despite the visible scars, I felt more comfortable, more accepting of my body. There, in the mirror, was all that I'd worked for. *I did it,* I thought. Blemishes and all, it was earned, and it was mine. Removing the skin brought me closure.

And I respected what remained.

11

WHEN WINTER CAME AGAIN AND MY BODY HAD HEALED,
I returned to film. Lori called on a Tuesday in February to ask if I'd
be interested in working on a movie with her in Philadelphia. I
barely let her finish the question before shouting "Yes!"

I heard her smile into the phone. "Great! Can you be there in
a week?"

Uh, no.

"Yes!" was what came out of my mouth. I hung up the phone
and immediately dialed Daniel, who was away at a poker tourna-
ment in Connecticut. He hadn't yet said hello when I started. "I
talked to Lori. We need to move to Philadelphia. At the end of this
week. How's that sound?"

As he often did, he waited and told me calmly, "Kiddo, first
breathe."

I breathed, thankful for the reminder.

"Okay. Now tell me."

I told him what few details I knew of the film I'd just committed to. "It's a James Brooks romantic comedy set to star Reese Witherspoon, Owen Wilson, Paul Rudd, and Jack Nicholson. Lori needs me to be her right hand in the art department in Philly. I told her I can start this Monday."

He waited for what seemed like a full minute before replying, "Okay, but . . ." I feared what rational argument would follow. We had discussed moving in together, but not this soon.

"We have a lot of work to do," he said.

I loved that his calm could temper my mania without stifling it. I yammered quickly into the phone, pacing around my bedroom assessing what I'd bring. "I'll get us a U-Haul. I think just the ten-foot one will work, right? Anyway, I can have my stuff packed by tomorrow. I'll just need to cancel my gym membership, see if Mom can get Friday off from work, and, I mean, I guess that's it. I really hate to leave Kate. Jesus, I'll miss her something fierce."

He cut me off. "Hey hey hey—slow down. I don't know if I can go that fast. I'll need to try to get out of my lease first. I might not be able to join you right away."

I thought for a moment. I breathed deeply and said, gently, "Please."

I waited for him to say something, anything. I could hear him breathe as he mulled it all over. Finally, he said, "We'll go," and "I'll do everything I can."

"Thank you, thank you, thank you, thank you, thank you!" I gushed.

Before the sun even rose that next Saturday morning, we were en route to Philly, a U-Haul of my belongings towed behind Mom and me in her Corolla. I hadn't yet secured an apartment. In fact,

I hadn't planned much of anything. All I knew was that we were headed eight hours south, and I'd be starting a new film job come Monday at eight a.m. Daniel, still tying up the loose ends of his life in Cambridge, was set to come to Philly and join me in our yet-to-be-found apartment in a week's time.

Somehow in the span of two days, I found an apartment, signed a six-month lease, and bought a bed, a couch, and the contents of the local Target. It was all possible because of Daniel, who had wired me enough money to pay for our lease up front, thereby expediting a process that usually takes longer than a weekend. Not until I could pay him back fully, years later, would there ever be enough ways to thank him.

I loved Philly. It was an adventure, exhilarating and frenzied. Lori and I became even closer, spending twelve hours a day by each other's side, talking as though we'd never run out of things to say.

After work and on weekends, I cooked. Fiendishly. For the first time, I had my own kitchen, my very own home. I had a chance to make a family or, at the very least, to compensate for the lost years when I felt I didn't have one—the years I ate cereal alone. I had Daniel, to cook for and eat dinner with nightly. I also knew that my preparing healthy, light meals could help him reach his goal of losing the hundred-plus pounds he wanted to lose. Despite his many weight loss attempts over the years, he struggled with consistency. I could see the way his weight burdened him, how intensely self-conscious he'd become, and how desperately he tried to conceal both his eating and his size. Having been in the same position just a few short years earlier, I understood his feelings all too well. I cared deeply about Daniel's well-being. I wanted him to be not only healthier, but happier, too. I viewed living together as my chance to kind of guide his eating, to get him to love the taste of wholesome foods. The way I'd cook for him would be the same way I cooked for myself: high in flavor and nutrients but lower in calories.

I kept our fridge stocked with more than enough healthy fare for just the two of us. Seasonal fruits, vegetables, organic yogurts, lean meats, and stinky, aged cheeses—all pure, real foods. I'd pull recipes from magazines, cookbooks, and blogs, and I'd hole up in the kitchen for an entire Saturday, cooking for hours on end. Mexican, Asian, Italian, American. A walk through my small kitchen was a food crawl in itself. On the stove bubbled marinara with Paul's famous meatballs that I made lighter with lean ground sirloin; on the counter to its left, a platter of chipotle pulled chicken breast; beside that, sweet roasted broccoli; and then a homemade whole grain pizza topped with grilled vegetables, crumbled goat cheese, and a drizzle of syrupy balsamic vinegar. I'd tuck all the foods into their own plastic containers, and we'd feast on delicious, wholesome meals for a week—leaving weeknights, when I'd arrive home from work at seven thirty, free to reheat and relax.

The recipe creation and the play of flavors filled me far beyond the dishes themselves. Seeing Daniel content and losing weight, week after week, was a satisfaction of an even higher level. I loved the hours in the kitchen. The preparation, the eating—they were cathartic. And despite the volume, I wasn't tempted to binge. I didn't fight a desire to gobble up the full pan of lasagna. Since I was the one making the meals, I didn't have to quell an urge to freak out at the calories. Instead, I felt calmer and more at ease. I prepared our food to be as balanced as I had begun to feel. I had learned to cook nourishing meals for myself and the man I loved, and in the process, I was making peace with food.

I experimented. Sometimes I failed miserably. But making the dishes I had always loved, in a way that felt nutritious, was worthwhile. Satisfying. Even the failures. I thought back to the buffalo chicken pizzas Daniel and I shared in my first college dorm, the white paper boxes of Chinese food littered around the table at home in Medfield, and every celebration with thick wedges of sour cream fudge cake. *There can be a life for these beloved eats,* I promised.

I stood there in my first kitchen, eight hours away from my mother, the one who breathed life into my cooking lungs, and I cooked. And when I was done cooking, I baked. Then I baked again. Because I loved it. And I wasn't myself without it.

The people on-set would have confirmed my obsession with cooking and baking. It really got out of hand after that first week. What began as "a simple sweet treat" for my coworkers turned into homemade Oreos, congo bars, and oatmeal cream pies. The bake shop I set up in the production office on that first day proved a hit. Within thirty minutes, a line had formed to my own little craft service station, and the goodies disappeared quickly. I did it again and again, bringing in a new treat each day. Lemon-scented black-and-white cookies, double coconut cupcakes, cheesecake in every flavor. In the end, I baked for sixty days straight.

It was then that I began to feel an urgency to share my recipes. I'd been reading food blogs for a few years, and as much as I loved lurking on sites and comment sections, there was a gentle itch to create my own. Daniel, who had lost twenty-five pounds while eating my healthy cooking, thought it was a great idea and pressed me to act on it.

As the film wrapped in late October, I contemplated my next move. Our six-month lease was two weeks from ending, and I hadn't yet heard of another available film job. Daniel recommended that I take advantage of the free time to start that blog.

Given how passionate I'd become about cooking, I started wondering if working in the film business was something I wanted to continue pursuing. "I'm not sure I love it like I used to," I told Daniel. "And it consumes so much of my life." The hours seemed unending. *Can I really keep going down this path if I'm no longer certain it's the one for me?*

Lori had warned me of this. Since the beginning, she gently tried to push me out of film production. Funny, given how I'd followed her states away for another film job. What she wanted for me, she urged, was more, better. She feared that I'd get caught up in moving from film to film, losing years of my life before realizing that I hadn't done anything else—anything more creatively fulfilling. She knew I craved more artistic control. And not simply in film; I loved so many things. To stay in this business, I'd be turning my back, at least for a while, on the possibility of other careers.

"You're young, Andrea. Explore other things. Now. Listen, I know you're going to be successful. I'm sure of it. And film—I mean, film will always be here. You can always come back."

She had a point. And I did want to try other things. I wanted to cook and bake and write recipes. I wanted to do more in the world of health and weight loss.

I mulled it all over. And then I got a call from Lori one evening, only an hour after I'd left her at the office. "Look, I'm not asking because I think you should come with me; I'm just letting you know because you're the only person I'd want to offer this job to." She breathed in. "I've been called for another job—a thriller in Connecticut. It starts in a week. You can do it with me, but you know . . ." She paused. "I just think . . . I just want you to try something else, something better. Get out of this shit business."

I felt blindsided. I was looking forward to a break. I wanted to spend the month of November thinking about what I wanted to pursue next. This news left me questioning everything.

"Just think about it. Get back to me tomorrow. You know I love you. Do whatever feels best." She hung up.

I talked to Daniel about it for two hours. We labored over staying, going, staying, going. And at the end of it, I'd made my mind up.

I would leave film.

It all sounded wild and terrifying. I had come to the conclusion that I would instead start a blog and try to make a living as a food and health writer.

That next morning, after barely three hours of sleep, I told Lori I wouldn't be coming with her to Connecticut. She hugged me, knowing that it was the best decision I could have made. I called Mom at the end of the workday and told her the whole ordeal—about the job and the blog idea. Talking it all through with her felt a world harder than coming to the decision on my own the night before. I knew how dearly she loved my work. It all sounded so glamorous to her—working on a big movie, with all the stars, moving from city to city. I feared her reaction to the news.

She sounded immediately tense. I could tell she was struggling. She remained silent for several moments, obviously still digesting the idea. Her reply of "Well, you have to do what you think is right" was quiet, strained, insincere.

My heart sank. Barely giving me a blessing to move forward with my plan, she said we'd talk more later. We hung up, and I instantly felt insecure about the whole thing.

Sitting on my bed, I panicked. *She didn't say it outright, but she doesn't think it's right. She wants me to take the job. To keep going.*

I called her back. No one's opinion affected me as much as hers. I couldn't bear the notion of her not agreeing with the direction of my life.

What began with me trying frantically to convince her of the merits of my would-be blog ended in a hysteria of crying and fighting.

"You can't turn your back on this business, Andrea." She'd never sounded so stern. "You have to realize how lucky you are to be doing what you're doing. This job is incredible, and you just can't see that right now. Listen, doing a blog isn't for you." I could tell she still didn't understand fully what a blog was. The way she spoke of it, I knew she thought little to nothing of a living made online. Certainly it paled in comparison with the Hollywood world. "You're not the type who can sit at a computer all day long. It's too reclusive for you. You're much too active for desk work like that." She did have a point.

Our conversation made me feel guilty. How dare I turn my back on a good thing? Choking on tears, I accepted her doubts about my choice. Eventually I relented. *She's right. I hate her at the moment, but she's probably right.*

My heart shriveled in defeat. We finally said good-bye, both of us angry at the other, and I walked into the living room. I admitted to Daniel, wearily, that I had reconsidered. I was going to accept the job in Connecticut. His eyes softened, his face pained to see my frustration. "Kiddo, you know, you don't have to. You're an adult now; you can do what you want to do. She'll understand eventually."

I pressed my lips together, the bottom one beginning to

tremble. "I know." I nodded. "But I care too much what she thinks of me. More than anything, I just don't want to disappoint her."

He sighed, knowing it was hopeless to try to convince me otherwise.

"And she's given me everything. I want her to be proud of what I've done with my life."

One week later I swirled my signature on the bottom line of a six-month lease in Hamden, Connecticut. Daniel and I looked at each other. How lucky I was that he'd up and move so often with me. As I looked into his eyes, my heart filled. *He's good to me,* I thought. He'd run clear across the earth if he thought it'd make me happy. The way he loved me was all consuming, unconditional.

How does he love me like this? I'd wonder. In the mornings, I'd wake to a new handwritten note. Something on the order of "Give 'em hell today. I love you"; or "I love you even though you have the biggest feet I've ever seen. Seriously, it's alarming"; or "I won't tell anyone that you chew in your sleep. They wouldn't understand. I love you."

I felt lucky that he had a profession that allowed him to move as often as I forced us to. Professional poker is good like that. In fact, it was on a trip we'd taken to Las Vegas for the World Series of Poker, just after we'd gotten back together, that I realized the extent of his love for me. Our second day there, my digital camera's battery died, so I resorted to snapping photos with Daniel's iPhone. Days later, nearing the end of our trip, he handed me his phone and told me to e-mail the pictures I'd taken to both of our Gmail accounts. Scanning the ones I'd taken during that week—dozens of fuzzy photos taken of food and pools and quasi-prostitutes—I found more I'd never realized he'd taken. Dozens of photos of an unknowing me.

At first I was taken aback by the rawness of a pajama-ed, wild-haired me. Unposed and unprepared. In the photos, I was doing everything from eating to reading to sleeping. I laughed as I thumbed through them. I looked terrible.

In one picture, I drank tea from a sixteen-ounce glass measuring cup. In another, I sat on our kitchen counter, eating frozen strawberries from a party-size bowl. Another showed me drinking water wearing a T-shirt Mom had bought me as a souvenir from a trip. The shirt read "Somebody who loves me very much went to Canada and got me this shirt." *Priceless.* In yet another photo, I crouched on the kitchen floor, smiling and looking crazy-eyed through the glass door of the oven to watch cupcakes rise.

And then I realized that these photographs were quite special. Because they captured the days I didn't think to document. Those times that went unmentioned, seemingly irrelevant in the grand scheme of things. Somehow they spoke volumes about my identity. Random images taken throughout the last year. They didn't have stories and archived memories; they were simply the in-betweens of my life. Each was weird but also revealing.

What was most interesting about those photographs wasn't that they were a sneak peek inside my daily life, but that Daniel found my life worth documenting. Not what I looked like or what I was doing in particular, but my zaniness. The quirks. The simple facts that I tuck my thermal pants into my socks and sit cross-legged in front of my oven door to watch my own baking projects.

In not even one photo was I dressed well. *What about that time I wore a dress?* Each was just something he found special somehow.

And now, looking through them all, I realized how lucky I was. He'd moved from Amherst to Cambridge to Philadelphia, and now to one forgettable town in Connecticut, just to be with me.

And I loved him for it. Because even when that Connecticut movie crumbled, when the production was abruptly shut down in January and I lost my job because the studio and the director couldn't come to an agreement on budget, Daniel smiled and offered reassuringly, "The bright side is that now you can start your blog."

The Monday that my first unemployment check arrived in the mail, I figured I had nothing to lose. I chose a free WordPress.com design, and *Can You Stay for Dinner?*—a name Daniel suggested—was born. At the beginning, I posted three times a day. I wanted to document the meals I ate daily to show how a person can lose weight and keep it off while still eating deliciously. It was to be a journal of my life through food. It was the long-winded answer to the questions I was often asked after losing weight. "How did you do it?" and "So . . . what do you eat?" and "What should I eat to lose weight?"

The challenge was avoiding health zealotry. I feared the self-righteous air that might exist on a blog that shares my path, my lifestyle. If I were to be too dogmatic, or if I set out a rigid list of diet rules, my message would be impractical and impersonal. For those reasons, I kept away from being too prescriptive when writing about weight loss. I needed readers to know that I was not a registered dietitian, not a licensed therapist, not aware of their unique complexities, their individual bodies, and, most glaringly—I wasn't even that good at turning down a cupcake. I was simply one person who happened to have lots of history and personal experience with dieting, losing weight, and learning to love her whole self.

So the blog was created with the sole intention to show rather than tell. Simply to be an illustration of me, painted colorfully in food. I hoped that the sharing of my reflections and recipes would mean something to others. I wanted readers to gain from what I'd lost, to develop an understanding of how I'd managed to change my life with food.

To do this, I asked them to stay for dinner. I invited readers into my home and showed them my breakfast, my salad at lunch, and my dinner, because I thought, *Well, I'm making it anyway, eating it anyway . . . might as well photograph it.*

I loved cooking and eating enough to snap an obscene number of photos of anything and everything edible in my home. I found something stylish, something sexy, in every picture, and I posted them for the world to see. I loved blogging immediately. The sharing, the give-and-take of commenting, the sense of community. A whole new world opened up.

I knew I had things to say about gaining and losing and maintaining that others might want to hear. And I knew that the things I'd say would not always make sense, not always be valuable to everyone. But I also knew that, at the very least, putting my feelings out there would be therapeutic.

And so I blogged every day. Before long, I began to receive comments and e-mails that made me glow from the inside out. Strangers told me their stories about food and weight; they related to me; they thanked me for putting myself out there in such a vulnerable way. The conversation, the staying for dinner—it made me the happiest I'd ever been.

Two months into the blog, our lease in Connecticut was nearing its end. I was committed to blogging, and I wanted the next job I took to be in line with food and writing. Daniel and I debated where to move next. San Francisco? Too expensive. Chicago? Too central, too landlocked. Down south? Too polite, too hot. And then Seattle came to mind. Our friend Justin had moved out there after college. He'd fallen in love with a girl, and they'd chosen to spend a few years in the Pacific Northwest, where she was from. He told us how fantastic it was.

I knew that the food culture there would be perfect for a wannabe food writer. For someone obsessed with cooking and all things edible, Pike Place Market would be a dream. Plus, I'd always had a fascination with the Northwest. I'd always wanted to travel west and live on the Pacific side of the United States, and this could be a great new adventure.

Weeks later, after selling all our belongings, we bought one-way tickets to Seattle. Telling Mom sent me into an anxiety attack. *What will she think? She won't like it . . . Am I making a mistake?* I went back and forth, thinking of all her reactions to life changes I'd made throughout the years since becoming an adult.

When I was eighteen, I pierced my nose. Mom lay in her bed and cried for two hours.

At nineteen, I told her I didn't want to pursue the honors track in college because "Who cares?" Mom lay in her bed and cried for two hours.

At twenty, I lost 135 pounds. Mom lay in her bed and cried for two hours.

At twenty-one, I told her I was deeply sad and didn't know how to go on. Mom lay in her bed and cried for two hours.

At twenty-three, I told her I'd just spent the night chatting with Leonardo DiCaprio and laughing with Mark Ruffalo on the set of *Shutter Island*. Mom was so excited and overwhelmed she lay in her bed and cried for two hours.

At twenty-four, I told her I was moving to Philadelphia to work on another film, but this time with Jack Nicholson and Paul Rudd. Mom lay in her bed and cried for two hours.

That same year, I told her I was going to stop working in film and start writing. A cooking blog. Not knowing what a blog was, Mom convinced me otherwise and then lay in her bed and cried for two hours.

At twenty-five, I called her to tell her I had sold my belongings and was moving to Seattle. *Just because I could and I wanted to and I'd already made up my mind.* Mom said, "Okay, follow your heart."

And I did.

She kissed me at the flight gate. "I'm so proud of you. Just remember, you can always come home." She fought back tears, as hard as I fought mine. I knew that at first she had only come around to the idea of blogging because I'd lost my job. She would never have consented for me to walk away from something stable, something more prestigious than cooking and clicking away at my computer—not when she knew what it was like to need a steady paycheck. But now, I had no other options. A month after I'd begun *Can You Stay for Dinner?* she called me to say "It's incredible."

"You mean that?" I asked her.

"I do. You're a writer, Andrea, and I guess I'm just figuring that out."

It was Mom and Paul who became my biggest fans—the ones who checked the site for updates three times every day, who called me constantly to comment, who told everyone they knew about it with pride. Paul would e-mail me a picture of a perfectly grilled steak with the caption "Thought this would be great for the blog!" while Mom would mail me pretty place mats and colorful dishes for food photography. Their support encouraged me to keep writing.

For the first time in quite a while, I felt secure. There I was, twenty-five, having lost a lot in life: my front teeth on the seesaw, my first spelling bee, my dad, 135 pounds, multiple pairs of sunglasses, and, most often, my way.

What I'd come to realize as I left for Seattle is that the gentle sensation of ants in my pants at all times is just letting me know I'm alive. That I'm on the verge. Of doing stuff. Or not. But just that there's something ahead.

I'm being reminded to take chances, to make illegal turns a time or ten, to crash, fail, and seriously consider a fallback plan at Starbucks.

I couldn't have said—in that moment or any other—that I always knew the right choice. I never did. I never do. I'd made Mom cry a thousand times. Salty joy and pain. But as I waved to her on my way through security, she and I both smiled.

12

SEATTLE WAS PRECISELY THE PICTURE that people painted it to be: mountains and water and nothing but lush, lush greenery. And hipsters. So many hipsters. And though the landscape took my breath away, it was the culture that I truly fell for. I found a life in and through and made of food.

When Daniel and I stepped off the plane with nowhere to live, we set up temporary residence at the Holiday Inn on Aurora. In the mornings, while Daniel slept, I'd venture out to some local coffee shop to blog. After a couple of days, I started browsing online for possible jobs. On Craigslist, an ad read, "Hiring a social media intern interested in food and writing." New to the whole social media scene, but proving adept at building a blog audience, I applied. Much of me felt certain I'd never get the internship, never even hear back from the company, Foodista, a two-year-old cooking website, though I loved the idea of working there. Surfing around the site, I was smitten. The design was clean and unpretentious. There was a question-and-answer forum where the community of users posted and answered food and cooking questions. And unlike other recipe sites I frequented, Foodista was a food encyclopedia as well. A Wikipedia of food, I'd come to realize five minutes into cruising its pages.

I assumed my luck would be similar to what it was with the slew of other jobs I'd applied for after graduating, which is to say, nonexistent. Surely they'd received résumés from dozens of people more qualified for the position. Still, it was worth a shot. After hitting Send on my reply, I went about exploring the Emerald City.

I'd all but forgotten about my application until three days later, when I checked my e-mail after a long afternoon walk with Daniel. In my Inbox sat a reply from the community outreach director at Foodista. An hour later, we were on the phone for an hour-long interview. Two days later, I was entering their building for an interview with the cofounder and CEO, Barnaby Dorfman. For nearly two hours, he and I sat in the open urban loft space and talked about the job, my work in film and his work with IMDb (the Internet Movie Database), our mutual fascination with the Pacific Northwest, the few years he'd spent living in New England while attending Dartmouth, his childhood in Manhattan, and all things food. We were alike in so many ways. Barnaby was down-to-earth and casual, and also very, very smart—almost exhaustive in the span of his knowledge. When I left the office, I was sure the meeting had gone as well as a meeting possibly could. I wanted the job more than I'd gone in wanting it.

On Monday, three days later, I was hired. On Tuesday, Daniel and I said farewell to suitcase living at the Holiday Inn and moved into our first Seattle apartment, sitting elegantly on the top of

Queen Anne's highest hill. And Wednesday I began what would be one of my most passionate career choices. Foodista was small enough that I felt at home in the office. I'd always considered myself a people person, but these people—my seven colleagues—were a rarity. Within my first few days of work, I'd settled into a delicious comfort with each of them. Barnaby, Sheri, Colin, Karlyn, Jesse, Patrick, and Jeff. They came to be my family.

After a month of proving myself to be a hardworking part of the team, I was promoted to a full-time staff member and assigned even greater editorial responsibility. I advanced from blogging once weekly to controlling all social media—everything from Facebook to Twitter. When the vice president of the company, Sheri, took her maternity leave, I was allowed a heavy hand in planning Foodista's renowned annual events, the International Food Blogger Conferences. For these, I sought out more than a dozen local chefs, restaurants, and even street food trucks to come and serve food during the weekend-long conference.

My work there fell neatly in line with all that I was doing in my personal life. The blog, the social media, the events—the fusion of passions couldn't have made more sense for me at the time. Each piece that I was working on synchronized with another. I'd also found a network of like-minded food friends. Seattle felt like destiny's gift, all of it existing in oddly perfect harmony. I was happy, intensely happy.

And the blog—my baby if ever I'd known one—grew. I fell deeper in love with writing. I poured my energy, all my eccentric intensity, into developing recipes, crafting stories, telling my own truth about weight loss and maintenance.

A few times a week, my coworkers and I would walk to one of

our favorite restaurants near the office for lunch. Often our cravings united for the tacos at Barracuda Taqueria—two small, fresh corn tortillas piled with limey cabbage slaw and plump sautéed shrimp, drizzled with avocado crema. When Mexican wasn't the vibe, we opted for Vietnamese. Steaming bowls of pho made with spicy pineapple- and beef-flavored broth, filled to the brim with vegetables and tofu, thin rice noodles, and topped with crispy bean sprouts, fresh Thai basil, and hot chili sauce. This exotic bowlful had become my go-to comfort food on the days when it poured down rain outside.

On weekends, I cooked with the same zeal I'd discovered in Philly and Rome. I went to the outdoor farmers' markets in Fremont and Ballard, finding kindred spirits in Seattleites, most of whom were as interested in organics and food ethics as I was. I loved seeing the fresh ingredients around me, especially the seasonal produce. It seemed as though everything I could want was grown locally in the Pacific Northwest. And I came to credit those vegetables that I bought every Sunday with helping me to be able to eat what I wanted.

In the process of losing and maintaining my weight, I had long thought that fruits and vegetables made eating healthy easier. It was their fibrous, filling nature. I tried pairing whatever meal I craved with a mound of vegetables. It mattered less what was gracing one side of my plate, and more that the other side was overpopulated with plants. But it wasn't until I arrived in Seattle that I discovered I could enjoy those vegetables all the time. There I found ones I loved and discovered new ways to make them delicious. Caramelized brussels sprouts, sweet early peas, grilled white corn on the cob, and roasted butternut squash. I didn't just quarantine a green on my dinner plate and promise to eat it for health's sake. I found out which vegetables tasted best to me, and which methods of preparing them made them as lovely as what I'd find in restaurants. And I experimented. I bought a new and different veggie each week. I used herbs and spices and introduced butter as a flavor rather than a foundation. I learned that roasting vegetables develops a sweetness without adding sugar. I was continually inspired to try out recipes and techniques, knowing that at least half the fun in cooking was the ideation beforehand.

Each night as I prepared dinner, I made it a point to balance that perfect square of cheesy lasagna, those two slices of my favorite homemade spicy caramelized-onion pizza, the chicken with mustard marsala sauce with at least double that of vegetables. When Daniel and I went out to eat at our favorite diner, the 5 Spot, I started with a salad and ate half of my burger, then shared my ancho-dusted fries with him. I brought my leftovers home for another meal. I felt content to eat whatever I wanted within reason because I didn't worry about whether a small portion would leave me hungry; the vegetables took care of that.

Every Saturday morning, I'd sit in the corner window of Starbucks on Queen Anne Avenue with a grande Americano and a bagel from Noah's, toasted as tan as is safe by toaster standards and spread with cream cheese. This breakfast was how I'd begin my weekend of cooking, writing, and food photography. And when I told a friend about my much-loved ritual, about the sunny spot in all my many Seattle Saturday mornings, she paused. She smiled, relieved. "I'm so glad to hear you like bagels. I eat them every now and then, but I always feel a little guilty about it."

I took a breath, not knowing if I'd been paid a compliment or been given a warning that bagels were calorie-laden carb bombs. I started scanning my memory of the previous day, the day before, and even the one before that, inspecting all that I'd eaten. What I ate, what I drank—they came to me in flashes. In between fruits, vegetables, crusty bread from Macrina Bakery, and a brownie from the pan I'd made for my coworkers, I noted that the bagel had hardly stood out as an exception to how I'd come to eat normally. I realized that her remark, in some small, indirect way, showed me how far I'd come in my relationship with food.

What I'd learned is that enjoyment and satisfaction can't always be quantified as energy input and output. Treating myself to foods and meals that might have put me in a caloric surplus did not make me fat, as I'd once feared they would. Intellectually, I always knew that all food was fine in moderation, but now the practical reality finally clicked. Bagels, as basic a food as they are, could be lovable to me because I was not eating them by the baker's dozen. Long gone were the days when I'd eat a bagel sandwich in the middle of the night along with a large fry and a doughnut, during a long drive with Sabrina in Amherst. I now made bagels special, like spaghetti and meatballs with Mom and Paul and popcorn with Melissa. They would have become mundane, no doubt, if I'd paid no mind to when or where or why I was eating them. The beautiful part about those doughy *O*'s was that I appreciated them most on Saturday mornings, eaten while sitting in my favorite coffee shop up the street. And when I'd finish my one bagel, I'd think, *Gracious, that was good.* And then I'd write. I'd put that bagel to work upstairs in my mind. And after a few hours had passed, I'd move on with my Saturday and my wide-open weekend, happy that I'd had my favorite breakfast on my favorite day, in my favorite corner of Seattle. I didn't regret it. I didn't spend precious mental energy considering what I might have eaten, what more I could have had for those calories I'd spent, how any plan of healthy eating has been ruined before noon—or worrying that a binge was awaiting. I'd just be left with the satisfaction.

This balance is what I've made of my life.

Without a scale in our apartment, I relied on the way my clothing fit to gauge if I'd lost or gained. Unfailingly, I seemed to remain the same, comfortably wearing a size four, depending on the store. Even though I ate a well-balanced diet and knew that I stayed within a healthy calorie range, since I could never truly forget about the numbers, I also knew that my active life played a significant part in helping me to maintain a steady weight. The mild climate in Seattle meant I could walk outside in all seasons. Our apartment in Queen Anne was close enough that I could walk to work at Foodista every day, often needing only rain boots and a light jacket. Each way was a mile and a half, with the return leg being a steep climb uphill, a feat that never failed to leave me lightly covered in sweat upon arriving home at night. In the afternoons at work, my friend Karlyn and I took breaks together, typically involving a trip to Starbucks five blocks away for coffee. On weekends, I took solo strolls around downtown, often popping into Pike Place Market to eye the flower carts and watch the fish being thrown for tourists. I took long Sunday hikes on scenic trails nearby. I met my new friend, Camille, to wander through the Sculpture Park and down along the Elliott Bay Trail whenever our schedules aligned. My car sat in the garage unused for long periods of time.

After two years of Seattle living, I sensed a marked change in my disposition. Life—something that had, just years before, felt so utterly dark, so difficult—was brighter, lighter. Food—something that had, years earlier, been best friend and enemy all at once—felt now purer, more sacred. My body—a source of tremendous inner turmoil for all the years I had known it—was whole and loved, by me. Still, there were certainly moments when life's stress would cause one or both sides of my eating disorder to reappear: the binger or the restrictor; those moments exist even now. But I learned to catch my predictable patterns sooner—before I fell too deeply into a bad cycle—and to treat myself with greater compassion.

What I failed to catch, though, was that as I continued to change and grow outward into a new career, a new environment, and new friendships, I was growing away from Daniel.

A year after we moved to Seattle, new government regulations severely limited Daniel's ability to continue his career. In April 2011, the federal government shut down the major online poker sites where Daniel played daily. His career in online poker was jeopardized and he stopped playing entirely while he figured out what he wanted to do. He began staying home all the time. And at first I understood. He'd always struggled with social anxiety. But then it became something else, in which he barely left. He fell into a deep depression. Seeing him that way, I'd plead with him to come out and meet the new friends I'd made: "We'll go for half an hour, tops!" Soon I ran out of excuses to tell my coworkers as to why he could never make it out for dinner or drinks after work. I'd have to muddle through arguments with friends who were hurt that my boyfriend didn't seem to care to meet them.

But the hard truth—the one that I prayed to be untrue no matter how viscerally I felt it, the one that crawled beneath my skin and gnawed at my bones—was that I'd fallen out of love. I felt as though I'd outgrown us—when really I'd just grown. I'd changed. And then Daniel withdrew.

There were always aspects of our relationship that had bothered me. The ways we differed—things one chooses to overlook, to accept, when in the throes of love. Only now I was less able to overlook them. Having spent seven years with Daniel, I was weary of them. I hated that he slept from three a.m. to twelve noon, which not only meant that I always went to bed and woke up alone, but that anything we did together in the daytime could not begin before midday. I struggled with his inflexibility. But of course, I had my own tragic flaws. In the moments when I was seconds from snapping at him, I reminded myself that he surely had a list equally long of things he disliked about me. I remembered when I was the most rigid and inflexible person on the planet.

None of the grievances mattered, though, when I was completely honest with myself. It wasn't the differences between us, not my wishing that he'd be less socially anxious, not my constant nagging and pushing him to be more ambitious. It was that I did not love him, romantically, any longer. And that was hard to admit, even to myself. I'd look at him, sitting on the couch in our apartment as I'd walk in the door from work at night, and I'd see my best friend.

The independence I'd cultivated in Seattle made me strong. Empowered. It made me believe that I could, indeed, do anything. The parts of my life that didn't bring me happiness anymore, just as a career in film hadn't two years earlier and my weight hadn't years before that—they were changeable. I had the right to find a new, authentic joy.

After a year and a half of living in Seattle and six months of arguing, I told Daniel everything I felt. Of all the good in our union, communication was always our strongest suit. We respected complete and utter honesty; we demanded it. And though he listened, I wasn't sure he could hear me. "Let's try to work on this," he said. I died, hearing the way his voice hitched. The honesty I shared with him during our hours-long conversations that summer of 2011 was painful, gut-wrenching. I cried, telling him things I'd fought to say aloud. Even if my falling out of love with him was true, I didn't always want it to be. I recognized how easy it could be if I could only just let us be as we'd always been. If we moved on to marriage, as we'd once discussed. If we continued in the comfortable routine we'd established. But that frightened me.

He tried harder. I tried harder. But nothing ever changed. *How do you leave your best friend?* I'd ask myself over and over.

Late that August, I attended one of the International Food Blogger Conferences I'd planned for Foodista in New Orleans. I spent a week in the Big Easy working, eating fried shrimp po'boys, and drinking hurricanes. Not once did I call Daniel while I was away, which was unusual. We always kept in touch when one of us was away. Just a year earlier, I wouldn't have thought twice about calling him every night before I went to sleep. But I didn't want to talk. Instead, I resorted to texting him quick, cold messages like *Really busy. Be home soon.* Later, on the plane ride back to Seattle, exhausted and thoroughly stuffed, a sense of dread settled over me. If I had a choice, home wasn't the place I'd go. Part of it was the natural comedown from the adrenaline rush I always experienced during a conference, but a larger part was knowing I hadn't missed Daniel. I didn't want to return to him, to us.

My taxi from the airport chugged up Queen Anne Avenue, the

streets shimmering with a slick of rain. As we turned right onto my street, the headlights lit my building in the distance. And I saw him. Standing on our front steps, he must have been waiting there for quite a while, since I'd only texted him a quick *I'm home* when I landed and not when I finally left the airport nearly forty-five minutes later. He smiled, there on our stoop. Behind the tinted glass of the taxi's window, my lips parted and my jaw dropped. I couldn't stifle an emerging sob. Here was a man who loved me endlessly. And here I was, not able to love him back. I knew then.

I broke up with him.

The days that followed were insufferable. Daniel uttered few words. He was icy, ghostly in the way he went about living normally. What little joy we might have had before was now entirely stripped away. I thought briefly to take it back, desperate to relieve us from the hellish existence I'd created. But then I thought of the relief that washed over me when I'd done it, when I'd finally said the words I'd been putting together in my head for half a year.

By late fall, Daniel had left our apartment and Seattle. The grieving, the unbearable weight of guilt, the emptiness—they brought me to my knees. And yet I knew it was right. This whole time of life humbled me. It made me see I didn't have it all figured out. Not with love, not with life, not with food. There were times, in the wake of our separation, when I turned back to food for comfort. When I overate the sweets I baked to fill the void of Daniel. And I was reminded, for the hundredth time in my life, as my belly ached and my heart raced from sugar, that food couldn't heal me.

It took a long time to feel normal again, to feel the familiar ease I'd developed with food and my body. In grieving the end of our relationship, I'd gained fifteen pounds. And, slowly, as I felt the balance restored, I accepted them as part of me. Maybe I'd lose them; maybe I wouldn't; either way, I had to be kind to myself.

What I discovered in that year—and perhaps in all of my life—was that I am always growing, always learning. And whenever I think I've figured it all out, I've really only just begun.

conclusion

I will always miss some aspects of life when I was big . . . 135 pounds ago.

I'll miss the reckless abandon.

I'll miss the volume of food, the horizon of eats that lay before me on a table, knowing full well that the only thing stopping me from consuming it all was my fist-size stomach. And even then there was always stretch.

I'll miss the way the fourth slice of pizza tastes. The fifth even more.

I'll miss bricks of brownie + ice cream + caramel + whipped cream + crumbles of a Reese's twosome. For a snack after lunch.

I'll miss when menus at restaurants were just lists of delicious dinners. And nothing more nutritionally threatening.

I'll miss not thinking before deciding that, why, yes, I'd absolutely adore three doughnuts for breakfast.

I'll miss plunging my forearm into a bucket of twice-buttered popcorn at the movie theater. Shoveling handfuls of salted and soggy kernels into my gullet. Then Sno-Caps. Then Sprite.

I'll miss brunching with sausage, egg, and cheese on greased and griddled everything bagels in the dining hall at college. With hash browns and a mind on lunch.

I'll miss all ten inches of that buffalo chicken pizza I called for when the party music stopped playing.

I'll miss not caring when or how my next meal came, only that it came. And stayed. And never left.

I'll miss the way Cap'n Crunch-ed so loudly, I couldn't hear my dad hollering.

I'll miss that feeling I had when every fiber of my anatomy believed food to be the kindest, most loving friend a girl could have.

And yet.

I won't miss the way heat felt suffocating. The way temperatures teasing seventy threatened me. And my hair.

I won't miss the Lucky Charms and the Corn Pops and the Honeycombs that helped me with my homework. They never helped me with my math equations when I'd begged them to.

I won't miss wondering if invisibility would be a more comfortable state. There are no places to live there.

I won't miss the way my legs chafed, the way shorts rode up until I discreetly tugged them down.

I won't miss the way my legs instantly fell asleep if I dared sit cross-legged on the floor.

I won't miss being a wallflower.

I won't miss watching people move, and act, and sing, and dance and wishing, oh, wishing, I felt that free.

I won't miss thinking, "Someday they'll see. I'm prettier than they know. One day . . ."

I won't miss my stomach calling my brain to tell her I'd eaten enough and I just couldn't (couldn't!) eat another bite. She never answered.

I won't miss the staring.

I won't miss the names—"fat" and "pig" and "whale"—and my ignored cries for mercy.

I won't miss the excuses and the regrets and feeling I'd wasted precious years. I won't miss the tears.

I won't miss dreading, oh, dreading, any occasion with dresses, or dressing up, or dressing at all, really. Not the girdles. Not the high heels that made my feet appear four sizes smaller than my body. The panty hose.

I won't miss thinking that size sixteen, eighteen, and twenty would fit differently, more acceptingly, in different stores.

I won't miss waiting.

And waiting. And waiting. Then waiting some more. For life to begin.

—›|‹—

When you're big for twenty years, the only twenty you've ever known, you'll kindly not frown upon two decades. You'll know that who you are was formed in there, and that's beautiful.

Quite simply, beautiful.

I read and hear accounts of others who've lost a tremendous amount of weight, like me. And most often, they speak about their former selves—the bigger ones—in a very detached way, as if the here and now is infinitely better and more lovely than the past. In many ways, perhaps it is.

But here's the truth I've come to know: fat or thin, it was me all along.

I don't think back on my past and want to redo it. I don't flip pages of my baby book and think, *Dear, what cankles you had!* I don't see my adolescent self, my teenage self, and wish those pictures, scrapbooked and framed, would disappear. *Mom, really, with the Glamour Shots?*

My life, big, was always all I knew. And that is perfect in its own right.

Yes, I know now that with 135 extra pounds, something more was wrong than just my weight. The scales I tipped should have tipped me off to emotional suffering. But not all of it was sad.

Some of the weight was happy and as well rounded as it came across.

Some of it meant that I developed a personality first. A sense of humor before a sense of entitlement. Empathy before ego. Some of the weight meant that I didn't care about myself. But in turn, maybe I cared deeply about a number of meaningful external parts of life. I poured my heart into relationships, molded it to fit friends and circumstances. A big ball, I rolled with the changes.

I found spirit.

I cared deeply about the way people perceived me. But maybe that made me more in tune and intuitive. Maybe because I was acutely aware of my size, I cultivated an awareness of all of life. Maybe I feel deeper, more purely and intensely. Maybe because my heart has ripped, and has lost pieces, and still has visible stretch marks and sewn seams, my character will be ultimately more resilient.

The thing is—it's easy to find the bad. I'm cynical at times. Pessimistic and realistic. I can, and do, look at situations in pros and cons. But what I've come to know as true, in the last twenty-eight years, is that I am everything I've ever been.

I will always know fat. And love who she was. And know that fat, in itself, is not a bad word. I'll own it and respect those twenty years. They were hard, but they were sweet, too. I grew up in that body, in that time, in that big, beautiful mind.

I will always know thin. And love who she is. And know that even when she feels heavier mentally, she's freer now. She's effervescent. Small but tough.

I will always know that the grass, though it seems emerald and glowing in that field on the other side—it isn't. Flowers grow here. They grow over there. Weeds do, too.

But both are wide, and they're open. And I can lie and cry in one and move and spin in the other, all while knowing this: they're the same field.

And they're both mine.

Sour Cream Fudge Cake
with simple chocolate buttercream

·›₁‹·

MAKES ONE 9-INCH LAYER CAKE, OR ABOUT 24 CUPCAKES

1 cup unsweetened cocoa powder

1 cup brewed coffee (hot)

½ cup sour cream

1 teaspoon pure vanilla extract

1 cup (2 sticks) unsalted butter, room temperature, plus more for the pans

1 cup granulated sugar

½ cup (packed) light brown sugar

3 large eggs, at room temperature

1½ cups all-purpose flour, plus more for the pans

1 teaspoon baking soda

½ teaspoon salt

Simple Chocolate Buttercream (recipe follows)

Preheat the oven to 350°F. Grease two 9-inch round baking pans with butter and line the pan bottoms with parchment paper. Grease the paper. Dust the pans with flour, and tap out the excess. Alternatively, for cupcakes, line two standard muffin tins with paper liners and spray the liners with nonstick cooking spray.

In a small bowl, combine the cocoa powder and the brewed coffee and stir until smooth. Let cool to room temperature. Stir in the sour cream and vanilla. Set aside.

In the bowl of a stand mixer fitted with the paddle attachment, beat the butter on medium-high until smooth and shiny. Add both sugars and beat until the mixture is fluffy, about 3 minutes. Add the eggs one at a time, beating for 30 seconds after each addition.

In a medium bowl, whisk together the flour, baking soda, and salt. With the mixer running on low, add a third of the flour mixture to the egg mixture, followed by a third of the cocoa mixture. Scrape down the sides of the bowl and repeat the process twice. Continue to beat on low until the batter is fully mixed, about 20 seconds more.

Divide the batter evenly between the prepared pans. Bake until a toothpick inserted in the center of each cake comes out clean, about 25 to 30 minutes (18 to 20 minutes for cupcakes).

Transfer the pans to wire racks and let cool for 20 minutes. Run a knife around the edges of each pan, invert the cakes onto the wire racks, and peel off the paper liners. Flip the cakes back over and let cool completely.

Put one cake layer on a plate and spread the top with 1 cup of the chocolate buttercream. Put the second layer on top and spread the top and sides of the cake with the remaining buttercream. The frosted cake can be covered and stored in the refrigerator for up to 3 days.

Simple Chocolate Buttercream

MAKES ABOUT 4 CUPS

4 cups confectioners' sugar

½ cup unsweetened cocoa powder

1 cup (2 sticks) unsalted butter, at room temperature

¼ cup whole milk

1 teaspoon pure vanilla extract

In a medium bowl, whisk together by hand the confectioners' sugar and cocoa.

In the bowl of a stand mixer fitted with the whisk attachment, beat the butter on medium-high until fluffy, about 1 minute.

Gradually add the sugar mixture, 1 cup at a time.

Add the milk and vanilla and continue to beat on medium-high until the frosting is light and fluffy, about 3 to 4 minutes. If it is too thick, add more milk, 1 tablespoon at a time.

The frosting will keep in an airtight container in the refrigerator for up to 1 week.

acknowledgments

Thank you, first and foremost, to the readers of CanYouStay forDinner.com. I wrote this book for you and am forever grateful to each and every one of you.

Ashley Phillips, this book would not exist without you. Thank you for every single painstaking hour you spent on it, and for loving me the whole way through. You are truly wonderful. Thank you, Doris Cooper, for taking a chance on me. To all of the kind, generous, and hard-working people at Clarkson Potter and Random House who took part in making this book a reality—especially Pam Krauss, Rica Allannic, Terry Deal, Ashley Tucker, Stephanie Huntwork, Heather Williamson, Erica Gelbard, and Carly Gorga—I am indebted to you. Thank you thank you thank you.

Steve Troha, thank you, 1. for believing in me, 2. for all of your dedication, and 3. for being a dear friend.

Melissa McMeekin, you started this thing. I won't be able to pay you back, but I'll always know it was you who helped me find this path.

Leslie Meredith, the fact that you even picked up the phone to speak with me, *wow*. Thank you for helping me to believe that I had something worth writing. I'm grateful to you.

Mom and Anthony, you two are my history, my heart. I love you as much as I know how.

Daniel, I love you more than anyone or anything, except the woman who birthed me (see Mom, above). I would not be here without you.

Dad, you did your best. I know that now. I love you. I miss you every day.

PJ, thank you for loving me unconditionally. You are the greatest dad I've ever known. I love you twice as much as I'm capable of expressing in words.

Kate Fernandes, seventeen years and we're still in love. Thank you for being my chosen sister. My life's partner. I love you endlessly.

Sabrina Peduto, I never imagined I'd find a best friendship like ours. The greatest years of my life have been with you. Thank you for unconditionally loving me.

Nicole, Katie, and C, thank you for accepting me and loving me as a part of your family—not just now, but always. I could not have asked for better sisters.

Claire Mitchell, I couldn't have imagined a better wife for my brother. You are a gift to our family. Thank you for loving us even though we're all crazy.

The Dewey Family, thank you. I can't quite tell you how much I love each of you (especially you, Michael) for letting me be a part of your family. Also, Mike, thank you for writing my college entrance application letter. Please never tell anyone about that.

Barnaby Dorfman, thank you for always believing in me. Thank you for teaching me all that you could about blogging, about social media, about business, about life. . . . You are a true mentor and friend.

Sheri Wetherell and my old Foodista clan, thank you for every opportunity. You are my West Coast family.

Lori Kuzmanovic, my life changed when I met you six years ago. You gave me one hell of a chance. I met Leo! More than that, you and I now have this beautiful, amazing friendship. And I love you, always.

Camille Willemain, thank you for all that you've taught me. For the unending and unconditional love. For all the memories we'll always have.

Mr. & Mrs. F, my second set of parents, thank you. For all the dinners, all the drives, all the times I came to your house and never left. I love you both more than you know.

Leonardo DiCaprio, thank you for that one time when you humored me during *Shutter Island*. And for the photo. I'd post it here but, honestly, I look terrible.

To all the people I mentioned in the book, thank you for being a part of my life, my story.